INTERPOL
Security and Its Security Problems

INTERPOL
Security and Its Security Problems

Rajesh K. Jha

Prashant Publishing House
DELHI - 110094 (INDIA)

PRASHANT PUBLISHING HOUSE
C-34, 28 Foota Road, Gali No. 3
West Karawal Nagar, Delhi-110094
Phone : 9810396373, 22963970

INTERPOL : Security and Its Security Problems

First Published : 2008

ISBN : 978-81-906344-3-4

PRINTED IN INDIA

Published by Mr. R. K. Jha M/s. Prashant Publishing House, Delhi and Printed at H.S. Offset Press, Delhi.

PREFACE

INTERPOL recognizes the demand to present advances made in scientific methods and to look into future forensic needs and trends, by bringing together executives and senior scientists from crime laboratories and forensic services throughout the world, to evaluate on a regularly basis progresses made within a certain period. In this perspective the INTERPOL its Security and Security Problems is offering a comprehensive overview of key areas of forensic sciences during the previous three years and therefore allow managers to focus on the most relevant issues.

The objectives of the IFSS are to provide a forum for forensic managers from member states to facilitate:

(a) the presentation of advances made in scientific methods over the previous three (3) years, and to provide a look into future forensic needs and advances,

(b) the exchange of information which will enhance scientific methods in criminal investigation and the administration of justice,

(c) the discussion of problem areas encountered by member states and the possible provision of solutions, and

(d) the exchange and pooling of ideas for future progress

This book provide complete overview and history of INTERPOL. I hope that readers will find it beneficial and informative.

— ***Editor***

CONTENTS

1

INTERPOL : INTRODUCTION

INTERPOL is the world's largest international police organization, with 186 member countries. Created in 1923, it facilitates cross-border police cooperation, and supports and assists all organizations, authorities and services whose mission is to prevent or combat international crime.

INTERPOL aims to facilitate international police cooperation even where diplomatic relations do not exist between particular countries. Action is taken within the limits of existing laws in different countries and in the spirit of the Universal Declaration of Human Rights. INTERPOL's constitution prohibits 'any intervention or activities of a political, military, religious or racial character.'

INTERPOL'S LEADERSHIP

The President of INTERPOL and the Secretary General work closely together in providing strong leadership and direction to the Organization.

As defined in Article 5 of its Constitution, INTERPOL (whose correct full name is 'The International Criminal Police Organization - INTERPOL') comprises the following:

- General Assembly
- Executive Committee

- General Secretariat
- National Central Bureaus
- Advisers

INTERPOL's Structure

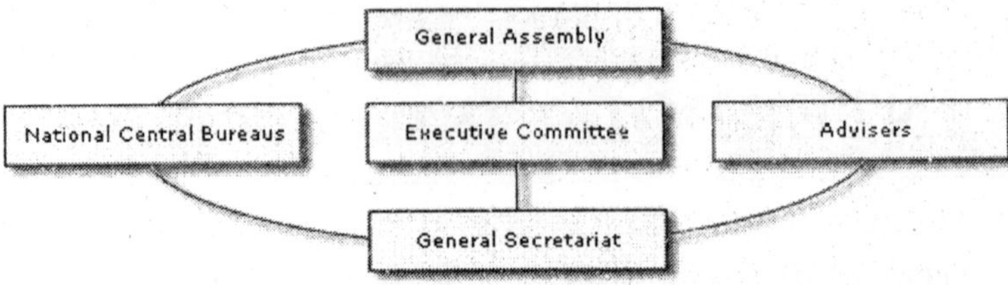

The General Assembly and the Executive Committee form the organization's Governance.

General Assembly - INTERPOL's supreme governing body, it meets annually and comprises delegates appointed by each member country. The assembly takes all important decisions related to policy, resources, working methods, finances, activities and programmes.

Executive Committee - this 13-member committee is elected by the General Assembly, and comprises the president, three vice-presidents and nine delegates covering the four regions.

General Secretariat - located in Lyon, France, the General Secretariat operates 24 hours a day, 365 days a year and is run by the Secretary General. Officials from more than 80 countries work side-by-side in any of the organization's four official languages: Arabic, English, French and Spanish. The Secretariat has six regional offices; in Argentina, Cote d'Ivoire, El Salvador, Kenya, Thailand and Zimbabwe, and a liaison office at the United Nations in New York.

National Central Bureaus (NCB) - Each INTERPOL member country maintains a National Central Bureau staffed by national law enforcement officers. The NCB is the designated contact point for the General Secretariat, regional offices and other member countries requiring assistance with overseas investigations and the location and apprehension of fugitives.

Advisers - these are experts in a purely advisory capacity, who may be appointed by the Executive Committee and confirmed by the General Assembly.

INTERPOL

The International Criminal Police Organization, better known by its telegraphic address Interpol, is an organization facilitating international police cooperation. It was established as the International Criminal Police Commission in 1923 and adopted its telegraphic address as its name in 1956. It should not be confused with the International Police, which takes on an active uniformed role in policing war-torn countries.

Interpol is the world's fifth-largest international organization in terms of the number of member countries, after the Universal Postal Union, FIBA (the International Basketball Federation), the United Nations, and FIFA (Football's international governing body). Its membership of 186 countries provides finance of around US$59 million through annual contributions. (By comparison, Europol receives $90 million annually.) The organization's headquarters are in Lyon, France. Its current Secretary-General is Ronald Noble, formerly of the United States Treasury. Noble is the first non-European to hold the position of Secretary-General. Jackie Selebi, National Commissioner of the South African Police Service, was president from 2004 but resigned on January 13, 2008.

In order to maintain as politically neutral a role as possible, Interpol's constitution forbids its involvement in crimes that do not overlap several member countries, or in any political, military, religious, or racial crimes. Its work focuses primarily on public safety, terrorism, organized crime, war crimes, illicit drug production, drug trafficking, weapons smuggling, trafficking in human beings, money laundering, child pornography, white-collar crime, computer crime, intellectual property crime and corruption.

In 2005, the Interpol General Secretariat employed a staff of 502, representing 78 member countries. Women comprised 42 percent of the staff. The Interpol public website received an average of 2.2 million page visits every month. Interpol's red notices ("difusiones rojas") that year led to the arrests of 3,500 people.

HISTORY

Interpol was founded in Austria in 1923 as the International Criminal Police (ICP). Following the Anschluss (Austria's annexation by Nazi Germany) in 1938, the organization fell under the control of Nazi Germany and the Commission's headquarters were eventually moved to Berlin in 1942. It is unclear, however, if and to what extent the ICPC files were used to further the goals of the Nazi regime.

After the end of World War II in 1945, the organization was revived, as the International Criminal Police Organization, by European Allies of World War II officials from Belgium, France, Scandinavia and the United Kingdom. Its new headquarters were established in Saint-Cloud, a town on the outskirts of Paris. They remained there until 1989, when they were moved to their present location, Lyon.

METHODOLOGY

Each member country maintains a National Central Bureau (NCB) staffed by national law enforcement officers. The NCB is the designated contact point for the Interpol General Secretariat, regional bureaus and other member countries requiring assistance with overseas investigations and the location and apprehension of fugitives. This is especially important in countries which have many law-enforcement agencies: this central bureau is a unique point of contact for foreign entities, which may not understand the complexity of the law-enforcement system of the country they attempt to contact.

For instance, the NCB for the United States of America is housed at the United States Department of Justice (DOJ). The NCB will then ensure the proper transmission of information to the correct agency.

Interpol maintains a large database charting unsolved crimes and both convicted and alleged criminals.

At any time, a member nation has access to specific sections of the database and its police forces are encouraged to check information held by Interpol whenever a major crime is committed. The rationale behind this is that drug traffickers and similar criminals have international ties, and so it is likely that crimes will extend beyond political boundaries.

Since 2002, Interpol has also been maintaining a database of lost and stolen identification and travel documents allowing member countries to validate whether a document issued by another country has been invalidated by the issuing authority due to being reported missing or stolen. Passport fraud, for example, is often performed by altering a stolen passport, thus several countries are working on integrating online queries to this database into their standard border control procedures to help identify fraudulent passports from foreign countries when those passports are presented. As of early 2006, the database contained over ten million identification items reported lost or stolen and is expected to grow even more as more countries join the list of those reporting into the database.

A member nation's police force can contact one or more member nations by sending a message relayed through Interpol offices.

MEMBER STATES AND SUB-BUREAUS

Sub-bureaus shown in *italics*.

Afghanistan	Cyprus
Albania	Czech Republic
Algeria	Denmark
American Samoa	Djibouti
Andorra	Dominica
Angola	Dominican Republic
Anguilla	East Timor
Antigua and Barbuda	Ecuador
Argentina	Egypt
Armenia	El Salvador
Aruba	Equatorial Guinea
Australia	Eritrea
Austria	Estonia
Azerbaijan	Ethiopia
Bahamas	Fiji
Bahrain	Finland
Bangladesh	France
Barbados	Gabon
Belarus	Gambia
Belgium	Georgia
Belize	Germany
Benin	Ghana
Bermuda	*Gibraltar*
Bhutan	Greece
Bolivia	Grenada
Bosnia and Herzegovina	Guatemala
Botswana	Guinea
Brazil	Guinea Bissau
British Virgin Islands	Guyana
Brunei	Haiti
Bulgaria	Honduras
Burkina Faso	*Hong Kong*
Burundi	Hungary
Cambodia	Iceland
Cameroon	India
Canada	Indonesia
Cape Verde	Iran
Cayman Islands	Iraq
Central African Republic	Ireland
Chad	Israel
Chile	Italy
China (PRC)	Jamaica
Colombia	Japan
Comoros	Jordan
Republic of the Congo	Kazakhstan
Democratic Republic of	Kenya
Congo	Kuwait
Costa Rica	Kyrgyzstan
Côte d'Ivoire	Laos
Croatia	Latvia
Cuba	

Lebanon	Rwanda
Lesotho	St. Kitts and Nevis
Liberia	St. Lucia
Libya	St. Vincent and the Grenadines
Liechtenstein	São Tomé and Príncipe
Lithuania	Saudi Arabia
Luxembourg	San Marino
Macau	Senegal
Macedonia	Serbia
Madagascar	Seychelles
Malawi	Sierra Leone
Malaysia	Singapore
Maldives	Slovakia
Mali	Slovenia
Malta	Somalia
Marshall Islands	South Africa
Mauritania	South Korea
Mauritius	Spain
Mexico	Sri Lanka
Moldova	Sudan
Monaco	Suriname
Mongolia	Swaziland
Montenegro	Sweden
Montserrat	Switzerland
Morocco	Syria
Mozambique	Tajikistan
Myanmar	Tanzania
Namibia	Thailand
Nauru	Togo
Nepal	Tonga
Netherlands	Trinidad and Tobago
Netherlands Antilles	Tunisia
New Zealand	Turkey
Nicaragua	*Turks and Caicos*
Niger	Turkmenistan
Nigeria	Uganda
Norway	Ukraine
Oman	United Arab Emirates
Pakistan	United Kingdom
Panama	United States
Papua New Guinea	Uruguay
Paraguay	Uzbekistan
Peru	Venezuela
Philippines	Vietnam
Poland	Yemen
Portugal	Zambia
Puerto Rico	Zimbabwe
Qatar	
Romania	
Russia	

Non-member Countries

North Korea

Kiribati

Federated States of Micronesia

Palau

Samoa

Solomon Islands

China (ROC)/Taiwan

Tuvalu

Vanuatu

Vatican City

Secretaries-general and Presidents

Secretaries-general since organization's inception in 1923:

Oskar Dressler	to 1946
Louis Ducloux	to 1951
Marcel Sicot	to 1963
Jean Népote	to 1978
André Bossard	to 1985
Raymond Kendall	to 2000
Ronald Noble	since 2000

Presidents since organization's inception in 1923:

Johann Schöber	to 1932
Franz Brandl	to 1934
Eugen Seydel	to 1935
Michael Skubl	to 1938
Otto Steinhäusl	to 1940

Reinhard Heydrich	to 1942
Artur Nebe	to 1943
Ernst Kaltenbrunner	to 1945
Florent Louwage	to 1956
Agostinho Lourenço	to 1960
Richard Jackson	to 1963
Fjalar Jarva	to 1964
Firmin Franssen	to 1968
Paul Dickopf	to 1972
William Leonard Higgitt	to 1976
Carl Persson	to 1980
Jolly Bugarin	to 1984
John Simpson	to 1988
Ivan Barbot	to 1992
Norman Inkster	to 1994
Björn Eriksson	to 1996
Toshinori Kanemoto	to 2000
Jesús Espigares Mira	to 2004
Jackie Selebi	to 2008

INTERPOL IN POPULAR CULTURE

Contrary to what has been featured in some works of fiction, Interpol officers do not directly conduct inquiries in member countries. Its main role is the passing on of information, not actual law enforcement. As an international law enforcement agency, Interpol agents offer unique qualities that make them good candidates for fiction, even if such portrayals do not reflect reality.

Examples

- In the Sly Cooper series, Carmelita Fox and a few other characters are Interpol officers.
- Thompson and Thomson, detectives in the comic series The Adventures of Tintin, are Interpol agents.
- Inspector Gadget is an agent of Interpol.
- In the show Sealab 2021 Quin calls Interpol to find information on a fraudster named Master Lu.
- In the Lupin III franchise, Lupin's eternal foil, Inspector Zenigata, is an agent of Interpol.
- In the comedy film Johnny English, it is eventually revealed that Lorna Campbell is an Interpol agent spying on Pascal Sauvage.
- In Capcom's Street Fighter video game franchise (and many of its adaptations to other media), Chun-Li is an agent of Interpol.
- In Marvel's X-Men the now deceased Irish X-man Banshee was a former Interpol officer.
- In the movie Lord of War, Jack Valentine (Ethan Hawke) is an Interpol officer.
- In the movie Mission: Impossible III, Ethan Hunt (Tom Cruise) is told he is on Interpol's Most Wanted list.
- In the manga series Death Note, Interpol was trying to capture Kira, a vigilante killing international criminals.
- In the 2007 season of LOST, an Interpol report is seen when it is discovered that is has been filed against one of the main characters.
- In the book and movie The Da Vinci Code, Interpol

is mentioned several times, mainly in reference to their extensive database of information.

- In the anime Azumanga Daioh, the character Tomo Takino wants to be an Interpol agent in the future.
- The Goon Show made a few references to Interpol throughout their run in the 1950s.
- The logo of the Terran Empire within Star Trek's Mirror Universe resembles that used by Interpol.
- In the show Batman Beyond which takes place in the mid-21st century, Interpol is mentioned in reference to its criminal database.
- In the original Where in the World is Carmen Sandiego? game from 1985, the user worked for Interpol. Later Carmen Sandiego media instead featured the fictional Interpol-esque ACME Detective Agency.
- In the Indian movie Don starring Shah Rukh Khan, the Interpol is trying to capture Don.
- An American band shares the name Interpol.
- Department S was a British TV series about a fictional Special investigation department of Interpol.
- The protagonists in the film The Medallion are agents of Interpol.
- In the game Resident Evil: Code Veronica X, Chris Redfield from S.T.A.R.S. is working with an Interpol officer before he turns to Anti Umbrella Activism.
- Bryan Fury in Tekken 3 had been an American Interpol officer before he was turned to a cyborg after being shot by gunmen in a shootout in Hong Kong. Likewise, Lei Wulong is a Hong Kong Interpol officer.

- In Psych Shawn Spencer pretends to be an Interpol agent
- In Ocean's 12 the crew is handed over to Interpol agents
- In Vigilante 8: Second Offense Agent Chase works for CHRONOPOL, an Interpol for time.
- In the book Artemis Fowl: The Arctic Incident one of the antagonists notes to his companions that the protagonist, Artemis Fowl, has an Interpol file.
- In the movie Assassins an interpol agent is shot by Antonio Banderas
- In the movie Hitman, 2007, Agent 47 is chased by two Interpol agents.

CORE FUNCTIONS

INTERPOL's activities are all based on the following four core functions:

Secure Global Police Communication Services

INTERPOL runs a global police communications system called I-24/7, which provides police around the world with a common platform through which they can share crucial information about criminals and criminality.

Secure Global Police Communications Services

The ability of police to exchange crucial data quickly and securely is a cornerstone of effective international law enforcement. This is why INTERPOL developed the I-24/7 global police communications system.

The system connects the INTERPOL General Secretariat in Lyon, France, National Central Bureaus (NCBs) in member countries and regional offices, creating a global network for the exchange of police information and providing law enforcement authorities in member countries with instant access to the organization's databases and other services.

Member countries can also choose to grant consultative access to authorised law enforcement entities outside of NCBs, such as border control units or customs officials.

INTERPOL continues to develop new services and training programmes to ensure that users are able to make full use of the I-24/7 system. MIND/FIND technical solutions (Mobile and Fixed INTERPOL Network Databases) help countries access the system, by integrating into their existing computer-assisted verfication systems.

I-24/7 was created in 2003, with Canada being the first country to connect to the system. The final of INTERPOL's 186 member countries to join was Somalia, which was connected on 10 July 2007.

INTERPOL's Global Police Communications System: I-24/7

One of INTERPOL's core functions is to enable the world's police to exchange information securely and rapidly. The organization's I-24/7 global police communications system connects law enforcement officials in all 186 member countries and provides them with the means to share crucial information on criminals and criminal activities.

As criminals and criminal organizations are typically involved in multiple activities, I-24/7 can fundamentally change the way law enforcement authorities around the world work together. Pieces of seemingly unrelated information can help create a picture and solve a trans-national criminal investigation.

Using I-24/7, National Central Bureaus (NCBs) can search and cross-check data in a matter of seconds, with direct access to databases containing information on suspected terrorists, wanted persons, fingerprints, DNA profiles, lost or stolen travel documents, stolen motor vehicles, stolen works of art, etc. These multiple resources provide police with instant access to potentially important information, thereby facilitating criminal investigations.

The I-24/7 system also enables member countries to access each others' national databases using a business-to-business (B2B) connection. Member countries manage and maintain their own national criminal data. They also have the option to make it accessible to the international law enforcement community through I-24/7.

Although I-24/7 is initially installed in NCBs, INTERPOL is encouraging member countries to extend their connections to national law enforcement entities such as border police, customs and immigration, etc. NCBs control the level of access other authorised users have to INTERPOL services and can request to be informed of enquiries made to their national databases by other countries.

Operational Data Services and Databases for Police

INTERPOL's databases and services ensure that police worldwide have access to the information and services they need to prevent and investigate crimes. Databases include data on criminals such as names, fingerprints and DNA profiles, and stolen property such as passports, vehicles and works of art.

Operational Data Services and Databases for Police

To fight international crime, police need access to information which can assist investigations or help prevent crime. INTERPOL manages several databases, accessible to the INTERPOL bureaus in all member countries through its I-24/7 communications system, which contain critical information on criminals and criminality.

These include:

- MIND/FIND
- Suspected terrorists
- Nominal data on criminals (names, photos)
- Fingerprints
- DNA profiles
- Lost or stolen travel documents
- Child sexual abuse images
- Stolen works of art
- Stolen motor vehicles

Operational Police Support Services

INTERPOL supports law enforcement officials in the field with emergency support and operational activities, especially in its priority crime areas of fugitives, public safety and terrorism, drugs and organized crime, trafficking in human beings and financial and high-tech crime. A Command and Coordination Centre operates 24 hours a day, seven days a week.

Operational Police Support Services

INTERPOL seeks to enhance the role of NCBs and regional offices and increase the General Secretariat's responsiveness to their needs. This includes the development of emergency support and operational activities centred on the organization's priority crime areas: fugitives, public safety and terrorism, drugs and organized crime, trafficking in human beings and financial and high-tech crime.

The Command and Coordination Centre (CCC) operates round the clock in all of INTERPOL's four official languages (English, French, Spanish and Arabic) and serves as the first point of contact for any member country faced with a crisis situation. The CCC staff monitors news channels and INTERPOL messages exchanged between member countries to ensure the full resources of the organization are ready and available whenever and wherever they may be needed.

If a terrorist attack or natural disaster does occur, the CCC and the Crisis Support Group mobilise to offer and coordinate the organization's response. All messages and requests for information and assistance from the affected member countries are treated with the highest priority.

In addition, Incident Response Teams or Disaster Victim Identification teams composed of officers from the General Secretariat and member countries can be dispatched to the scene within hours of an event. The CCC can also assume a coordination role if an attack or disaster involves several member countries or if a member country's own ability to do so has been compromised.

Another component of this core function is the INTERPOL notice system, which serves to alert police of fugitives, suspected terrorists, dangerous criminals, missing persons or weapons threats.

There are currently six colour-coded notices- Red, Blue, Green, Yellow, Black and Orange - and the INTERPOL-United Nations Special Notice issued for groups or individuals who are the targets of UN sanctions against Al Qaeda and the Taliban.

The Criminal Analysis Unit contributes to investigations by assisting officers working at the General Secretariat and in member countries with research and analysis on crime trends. The unit also provides training courses in criminal analysis techniques for member countries.

INTERPOL initiates and coordinates many police training programmes covering different priority crime areas, and aimed at enhancing the capacity of Member States to combat international crime. The courses are open to Law Enforcement Agencies.

Training and Development

INTERPOL provides focused police training initiatives for national police forces, and also offers on-demand advice, guidance and support in building dedicated crime-fighting components. The aim is to enhance the capacity of member countries to effectively combat serious trans-national crime and terrorism.

This includes sharing knowledge, skills and best practices in policing through INTERPOL channels and the establishment of global standards on how to combat specific forms of crimes.

TRAINING AND DEVELOPMENT

Building Law Enforcement Capacity

Training and development plays a key role in INTERPOL's overall mission to promote international police cooperation. The aim is to help officials in INTERPOL's 186 member countries to improve their operational effectiveness, enhance their skills and build their capacity to address the increasingly globalised and sophisticated nature of criminality today.

INTERPOL offers many tools and services - for example, databases - to its member countries. To ensure that members can fully understand and use them, INTERPOL has launched a number of initiatives aimed at developing expertise and facilitating knowledge-sharing.

Following a sharp increase in demand for training from

member countries, INTERPOL assigned Training and Development as its fourth core function in 2007.

Objectives

The strategic objectives for INTERPOL's training activities for 2007-2009 are as follows:

- Enhance the capacity of member countries to combat global, international and regional crime by developing, facilitating and coordinating training initiatives in accordance with INTERPOL's priorities and key activities;
- Ensure that law enforcement agencies are fully aware of and take advantage of the services provided by INTERPOL;
- Develop best practices and global standards in policing by providing opportunities for the effective sharing of training materials, including support services, core competencies and expertise among member countries;
- Enhance the awareness, knowledge and skills of INTERPOL staff through a structured training programme, including in due course, developmental training;
- Engender a learning culture within INTERPOL that binds the organization together through a shared understanding of its values, purposes, core businesses and processes.

Sharing Knowledge among Member Countries

National Central Bureaus (NCBs) are INTERPOL's link with national police forces and they are increasingly called upon to play a greater operational role as INTERPOL expands the range of its activities and services. The General Secretariat needs to be in a position to assist them in dealing with international policing requests. To help coordinate training to those countries which need it, the capacities of INTERPOL's Sub-Regional Bureaus (SRBs) are being strengthened in collaboration with regional police chiefs' bodies and other organizations.

Each bureau has been equipped with modern training facilities, and the role of SRBs is currently being examined with a view to enhancing their training services.

To facilitate cooperation and expertise-sharing among member countries, INTERPOL has launched an initiative whereby countries can advertise their training courses on its restricted web site for NCBs and invite other member countries to participate.

Core competency guidelines for NCB staff are being developed by a group of NCB volunteers representing each of INTERPOL's regions, together with three representatives from the General Secretariat. The guidelines will outline the five main areas of competencies required of NCB staff.

INTERPOL is exploring opportunities with member countries to establish training institutions that can address priority crime areas or other areas of high concern. An INTERPOL Anti-Heroin Smuggling Training Centre was recently established in Moscow, and an INTERPOL Anti-Corruption Academy is being created in Austria.

INTERPOL'S TRAINING PROGRAMMES

INTERPOL Guide for Effective Training

The INTERPOL Guide for Effective Training explains how training needs are identified and assessed, the steps required to design, plan and implement quality training programmes, and how evaluations and assessments should be conducted. Aimed at police leaders and officers involved in police training, this comprehensive guide is available on the NCB Dashboard.

Annual Police Training Plan

The annual Police Training Plan lists operational training courses delivered or coordinated by the General Secretariat, and is available to all member countries via the NCB Dashboard. In 2006, 52 training programmes were delivered, benefiting 1,113 participants from 169 countries, while in 2007, around 60 police training programmes or workshops will be delivered.

INTERPOL International Police Training Programme

INTERPOL has developed an advanced 10-week training programme for police officers from law enforcement agencies and National Central Bureaus. It is aimed at officers with responsibility for international police cooperation, using the NCB network and working with INTERPOL's systems and services.

Participants - who should be officers of sufficient rank to bring about change and improvement upon return to their respective administrations - gain knowledge and skills through training and hands-on experience by working at the General Secretariat. Three sessions were conducted in 2007 and dates for courses in 2008 will be made available on the NCB Dashboard.

Internal Training for General Secretariat Staff

INTERPOL has a responsibility to ensure that all staff members are fully trained to perform their duties effectively and efficiently. Competency-based training is being adopted with the identification and establishment of core competencies for staff. In addition, continuity and "organizational memory" is being established through the sharing of knowledge.

Recommendations for Future Projects

The 16th INTERPOL Symposium for the Heads of Police Training held in Johannesburg in March 2007 adopted several recommendations, including the following:

1. To establish a working group to study the creation of a global INTERPOL Learning Management System (ILMS), including: a directory of experts that member countries could refer to for consultation; a library of e-learning packages and training programmes for member countries to share their training resources; and a depository of research papers and best practices to facilitate the exchange of information.
2. To encourage member countries to incorporate training modules on INTERPOL and its services into appropriate training programmes at police institutions and NCBs.

DRUGS AND CRIMINAL ORGANIZATIONS

Drugs

Drug abuse and the problems associated with it continue to grow in most parts of the world. The global abuse of drugs and the drug trafficking situation is becoming more complex, in part due to political and economic changes around the world which have led to increasingly open borders between many countries. These include:

- the emergence of a more affluent class of drug abuser with higher disposable income to spend on so-called 'recreational' drugs;
- a rise in demand and availability for almost all types of controlled substances;
- cultural changes brought about by globalisation and rapid communications.

The drug trade involves growers, producers, couriers, suppliers, dealers and users and affects people in almost all of INTERPOL's 186 member countries.

Drug trafficking is frequently linked to other serious crimes such as people smuggling, organized prostitution and travel-document counterfeiting. It is often cited as a means to finance the more violent and destructive activities of criminal and terrorist organizations, because of the major cash benefits derived from relatively minimal time and investment.

INTERPOL's primary drug-control role is to identify new drug trafficking trends and criminal organizations operating at the international level and to assist all national and international law enforcement bodies concerned with countering the illicit production, trafficking and abuse of cannabis, cocaine, heroin and synthetic drugs by:

- collecting and analysing data obtained from member countries for strategic and tactical intelligence reports and disseminating these reports to the concerned countries;
- responding to and supporting international drug investigations;
- helping to coordinate drug investigations involving at least two member countries;
- organizing operational working meetings between two or more member countries where INTERPOL has identified common links in cases being investigated in these countries;
- organizing regional or global conferences on specific drug topics, the aims of which are to assess the extent of the particular drug problem, exchange information on the latest investigative techniques and strengthen cooperation within law enforcement communities.

Interpol maintains close liaison with national law enforcement agencies and with Non-Governmental Organizations (NGO) that have a counterdrug mandate. Information gathered and assessed by these NGOs is valuable in creating a more comprehensive assessment of drug trafficking and abuse issues.

The United Nations Office on Drugs and Crime not only has information on drug trafficking and abuse studies, but reports on other criminal matters that have a global impact.

The World Customs Organization has information regarding the harmonization of customs controls and practices, and provides information on smuggling.

Criminal Organizations

Definitions of what constitutes organized crime vary widely from country to country. Organized groups are typically involved in many different types of criminal activity spanning several countries. These activities may include trafficking in humans, weapons and drugs, armed robbery, counterfeiting and money laundering.

INTERPOL currently has projects targeting organized crime in two areas of high activity: Eurasia (Project Millennium) and Asia (Project AOC - Asian Organized Crime).

FINANCIAL AND HIGH-TECH CRIMES

Financial and high-tech crimes - currency counterfeiting, money laundering, intellectual property crime, payment card fraud, computer virus attacks and cyber-terrorism, for example - can affect all levels of society.

Currency counterfeiting and money laundering have the potential to destabilise national economies and threaten global security, as these activities are sometimes used by terrorists and other dangerous criminals to finance their activities or conceal their profits.

Intellectual property crime is a serious financial concern for car manufacturers, luxury goods makers, media firms and drug companies.

Most alarmingly, counterfeiting endangers public health, especially in developing countries, where the World Health Organization estimates more than 60 per cent of pharmaceuticals are fake.

'Spam' is becoming more than just a nuisance for Internet users, as criminals are using it in increasingly sophisticated ways to defraud consumers, cripple computer systems and release viruses.

In 2000, the so-called 'Love Bug' virus, which affected millions of computers around the world within hours, exposed the vulnerability of corporate and government networks to such attacks.

New technologies open up many possibilities for criminals to carry out traditional financial crimes in new ways.

One notable example is 'phishing', whereby a criminal attempts to acquire through e-mail or instant messaging sensitive information such as passwords or credit card details by pretending to be a legitimate business representative. With this information, the criminal can commit fraud and even money laundering.

INTERPOL has stepped up its efforts in this area, working with stakeholders such as pharmaceutical makers, Internet service providers, software companies, central banks and other relevant bodies to devise solutions to thwart criminals and protect consumers.

INTERPOL's chief initiatives in the area of financial and high-tech crime focus on:

PAYMENT CARDS

The General Secretariat has played an instrumental role in helping law enforcement and industry partners around the world to address the growing problem of payment card fraud. As the use of payment cards continues to increase, it is likely that the frequency and extent of fraud will also continue to expand.

The payment card industry and law enforcement community are constantly working to develop enhanced production and security measures to deter payment card fraud, but criminals continue to devise more sophisticated methods to override such features. As a result, the need for communication and information-sharing has never been more important, and this is where Interpol can provide valuable assistance.

In the mid-1990s, the General Secretariat brought together various experts in the field for the First International Conference on Payment Card Fraud.

The Payment Card Working Group was established following the conference. Experts from the Hong Kong Police, Royal Canadian Mounted Police, United States Secret Service, UK National Criminal Intelligence Service, Netherlands National Police Agency and the payment card industry attended the group's first meeting. The representatives shared their expertise and established a classification system for payment cards.

A proposal for a central database to be housed at the General Secretariat was approved at the 66th General Assembly in New Delhi in 1997. By 2000, the database was established at the General Secretariat, and allowed for the classification of altered or counterfeit cards submitted by certified law enforcement and industry experts through forensic analysis.

The database is currently accessible to member countries and has proved to be a useful tool for the law enforcement community.

Recent Events

The General Secretariat has appointed a new forensic analyst to the Counterfeit and Security Documents Unit, which will continue to work with various partners to re-organize the database and the information it contains as part of Interpol's ongoing commitment to provide effective and relevant assistance to member countries.

Additional Information - Payment Card Security

To learn more about the ways consumers can protect themselves when using payment cards please visit the following web-sites:

- American Express
- MasterCard
- Visa.

FUNDS DERIVED FROM CRIMINAL ACTIVITIES

The international police community is aware that there is a need to achieve major results in the struggle against the financial criminal activities related to organized criminal groups. During recent years there have been a number of resolutions passed by the INTERPOL General Assembly which have called on member countries to concentrate their investigative resources in identifying, tracing and seizing the assets of criminal enterprises.

These resolutions have also called on member countries to increase the exchange of information in this field and encourage governments to adopt laws and regulations that would allow access, by police, to the financial records of criminal organizations and confiscation of proceeds gained by criminal activity (Resolutions AGN/55/RES/18, 1986; AGN/56/RES/11, 1987; AGN/60/RES/4, 1991; AGN/66/RES/15, 17 and 18, 1997).

Acknowledging the value of the 1988 United Nations Convention against illicit trafficking in narcotic drugs and psychotropic substances and the 1992 OAS Model Regulation concerning laundering offenses connected to illicit drug trafficking and related offenses, the Forty Recommendations of the Financial Action Task Force, the Convention on laundering, search, seizure and confiscation of the proceeds from crime (Council of Europe, 1990) and the European Council Directive on the prevention of the use of the financial system for the purpose of money laundering (Council of European Communities, 1991), the INTERPOL General Assembly meeting in New Delhi in 1997 called on member countries which have not yet done so to ratify the 1988 United Nations Convention against illicit traffic in narcotic drugs and psychotropic substances and to urge their governments to implement the Convention in order to give their law enforcement institutions the powers it provides for (Resolution AGN/66/RES/15, 1997).

Money Laundering - INTERPOL's Definition

A working definition was adopted by the INTERPOL General Assembly in 1995, which defines money laundering as: 'any act or attempted act to conceal or disguise the identity of illegally obtained proceeds so that they appear to have originated from legitimate sources'.

Working Group on Money Laundering and Terrorism Financing

The second meeting of the INTERPOL Working Group on Money Laundering and Terrorism Financing was held at the INTERPOL General Secretariat in Lyon, France, on

3 June 2005 and was attended by representatives from the Organization of American States, Offshore Group of Banking Supervisors, United Nation's Office of Drug Control, US Department of Treasury, Europol, International Monetary Fund, FIU.NET, EUROJUST and the UK's National Criminal Intelligence Service.

The meeting was preceded by a workshop concerning information-sharing between select NCBs and financial intelligence units (FIUs). Recommendations were made to:

(1) identify 'demonstration cases' involving NCBs which are already receiving money laundering information from FIUs;

(2) submit a resolution encouraging this type of cooperation to INTERPOL's General Assembly session in Berlin in September 2005; and

(3) seek formal recognition of the FIU/NCB relationships through incorporation into the Egmont Group's 'Principles of Information Exchange between Financial Intelligence Units'.

Presentations were made regarding surveys which will be launched shortly relating to cash couriers and alternative remittance systems. A proposal to expand the subgroup, both in terms of membership and by soliciting views from other policy-setting organizations, was unanimously agreed to by members.

Special progress was made in the training subgroup with the United Nations Office on Drugs and Crime (UNODC), which will organize training courses on money laundering in cooperation with INTERPOL.

Equipment provided by UNODC will be used during the training, which is planned to take place at the INTERPOL Sub-Regional Bureau in Nairobi.

The members decided that the next Working Group Plenary meeting will be conducted in conjunction with the 3rd INTERPOL International Financial Crime Conference, which will be held in March 2006 in Madrid.

IMoLIN Database

The Internet-based information network IMoLIN serves as a clearinghouse for money laundering information for the benefit of all national and international anti-money laundering agencies. It was developed and is administered by the Global Programme against Money Laundering of UNODC on behalf of the United Nations and other international organizations, including INTERPOL. There are five main features of IMoLIN, and all but one are accessible to the public:

AMLID (Anti Money Laundering International Database): Compendium and analysis of national anti-money laundering laws and regulations, as well as information on national contacts and authorities. The database is password-restricted.

Reference data: research and analysis, bibliography, conventions, legal instruments and model laws.

Country page: includes full text of anti-money laundering legislation where available and links to national FIUs.

Calendar of events: chronological listing of training events, conferences, seminars, workshops and other meetings in the anti-money laundering field.

Current events: current news of recent anti-money laundering initiatives.

International Meetings and Cooperation

The INTERPOL General Secretariat works closely with other international organizations to foster international awareness of the importance of utilising financial investigative techniques against organized criminal activities.

Most importantly, these liaisons and cooperation are aimed at supporting each international organization's efforts in these areas and avoiding duplication. The following is a list of international organizations which have participated in mutual cooperation and assistance in the development of international programs related to the assets of criminal organizations:

- Asia Pacific Group on Money Laundering (APG)
- Caribbean Financial Action Task Force (CFATF)
- Egmont Group
- European Banking Federation Fraud Working Group
- European Bank for Reconstruction and Development (EBRD)
- Financial Action Task Force (FATF)
- International Monetary Fund (IMF)
- International Organization of Securities Commissions (IOSCO)
- International Banking Security Association (IBSA)
- International Air Transport Association (IATA)
- Institut de Formation Interbancaire (INSIG)
- World Customs Organization (WCO)
- Inter-American Development Bank (IADB)
- Organization of American States/Comision Interamericana para el Control del Abuso de Drogas (OAS/CICAD)
- Offshore Group of Banking Supervisors (OGBS)
- Select Committee of Experts on the Evaluation of Anti-Money Laundering Measures (PC-R-EV Committee - Council of Europe)

INTELLECTUAL PROPERTY (IP) CRIME

Intellectual property (IP) crime is a generic term used to describe a wide range of counterfeiting and piracy offences.

Trademark counterfeiting and copyright piracy: involvement of transnational organized criminals

Trademark counterfeiting and copyright piracy are serious Intellectual Property (IP) crimes that defraud consumers, threaten the health of patients, cost society billions of dollars in lost government revenues, foreign investments or business profits and violate the rights of trademark, patent, and copyright owners.

Fake products pose a significant safety threat to consumers worldwide. Unsuspecting customers and patients put their health, and even lives, in jeopardy each time they use fake medicines, alcoholic beverages, food products and travel in automobiles or aircraft maintained with substandard counterfeit parts.

Transnational IP crime knows no boundaries and is evident all over the world. Evidence shows that transnational organized crime groups are actively involved in trademark counterfeiting and copyright piracy.

These crimes are linked with money laundering, the illicit trafficking of drug, firearms and other types of organized crime. In some instances paramilitary terrorist organizations have traded in counterfeit and pirated goods to maintain their organizations and fund their activities.

Worldwide losses caused by the involvement of transnational organized criminals in fake product manufacture and distribution are estimated to be hundreds of billions of dollars annually. The social, health and economic damages arising from the production and sale of fake products are substantial. There are many victims of transnational organized IP crime including people suffering from life threatening diseases who unknowingly use counterfeit medicines containing little or no active ingredients.

INTERPOL's Fight against IP Crime

There is an urgent need for national and international enforcement authorities to coordinate their efforts and cooperate with the IP right holders in the private sector.

Stakeholders in the fight against transnational organized IP crime are not just consumers, patients and IP owners, but also governments, the judiciary, the media and law enforcement authorities.

Law enforcement authorities including national police forces are at the forefront of collective efforts to combat the activities of transnational organized criminals. However, there is often a lack of trained investigators and the other resources needed to effectively address transnational organized IP crime. There is an urgent need for national and international enforcement authorities to coordinate their efforts and cooperate with the IP right holders in the private sector.

In October 2000, the INTERPOL General Assembly approved the addition of IP crime to the Organization's official mandate.

Shortly afterwards, the INTERPOL Intellectual Property Action Group (IIPCAG) was formed as a public-private partnership. Core membership of the Action Group consists of representatives from national law enforcement and customs authorities, international intergovernmental organizations, cross-industry private sector representative bodies and patent protection entities.

The Actions Group's mission is to provide an advisory group function; assist INTERPOL to develop strategies to combat transnational organized IP crime; and, encourage National Central Bureaus (NCBs) and national law enforcement authorities in INTERPOL member countries to dedicate more resources to IP crime enforcement.

INTERPOL's IP Crime Program

The INTERPOL IP Crime Program is constantly evolving to meet challenges posed by transnational organized crime. Combining the efforts of INTERPOL and INTERPOL's Intellectual Property Crime Action Group (IIPCAG) has broadened and strengthened partnerships with the private sector to improve the effectiveness of collective action to expand INTERPOL's capacity to tackle trademark counterfeiting and copyright piracy.

One of the objectives is to develop the Database on International Intellectual Property (DIIP) Crime to improve the exchange of information and intelligence on transnational organized IP crime. Designed to identify links between transnational cross-industry organized IP crime activity and other types of organized crime, the database is used to inform and facilitate law enforcement interventions in transnational organized IP crime.

IP Crime Program Objectives

- Develop strategies and programmes to combat transnational organized criminal activity linked to IP infringement
- Develop the Database on International Intellectual Property (DIIP) Crime to improve the exchange of information and intelligence on transnational organized IP crime
- Raise awareness among policy makers, stakeholders and the public about the central role of organized criminals in transnational IP crime
- Increase national and regional law enforcement efforts to combat transnational organized IP crime

- Develop a systematic worldwide operational capability to facilitate and coordinate regional enforcement action against transnational IP crime
- Provide police with support and training on IP crime

INTERPOL and the IIPCAG members work together in partnership to achieve these objectives. They also have identified the following priorities:

- Information exchange and maximizing benefits arising from DIIP
- The Database on International Intellectual Property (DIIP) Crime is designed to identify links between transnational cross-industry organized IP crime activity and other types of organized crime. It is used to inform and facilitate law enforcement interventions in transnational organized IP crime
- It will lead to the development of a systematic INTERPOL regional operational capability to facilitate and coordinate collective efforts to identify and disrupt transnational organized IP crime networks
- It will be used to produce regional and global strategic IP crime reports

It will improve the information flow between stakeholders and lead to more effective national and regional IP rights enforcement.

Development of Systematic INTERPOL regional Operational Capability

INTERPOL facilitates and coordinates regional law enforcement interventions in transnational and organized IP crime. Since 2004 INTERPOL has acted as a catalyst for interventions into transnational organized criminal activity in South America and South East Asia. Partnership action with national police and customs agencies supported by affected private sector entities has led to the arrest of hundreds of suspects and seizure of millions of dollars of counterfeit and pirate goods.

It has also led to the identification and disruption of a criminal conspiracy producing counterfeit medicines on an industrialized scale and undermining legitimate efforts by regional health authorities to cure patients suffering from life threatening diseases.

The development of the DIIP and increased flow of information for action will result in a more systematic INTERPOL regional operational capability to facilitate and coordinate law enforcement interventions in transnational organized crime.

Training

- Identify international operational and strategic training needs at national and regional levels
- Develop clear, consistent and specialized IP crime training programmes incorporating information from both the law enforcement community and the private sector
- Provide students and trainers with ready access to public and private sector training programmes and materials including the INTERPOL Guide to Intellectual Property Crime and Investigations

Contact Point

- Provide a central point of reference for transnational organized IP crime at the INTERPOL General Secretariat to facilitate contacts between law enforcement and industry IP Crime investigators
- Develop reliable support services for collective efforts

by IP crime investigators to combat transnational organized IP crime and improve communication

- Act as a collection point for information obtained from all available sources for input into DIIP to support regional law enforcement interventions into transnational organized IP crime

Public Awareness

- Formulate effective strategies to increase global awareness of the negative impact of transnational organized IP crime
- Identify key audiences and create communication programmes aimed at governments, law enforcement bodies, customs, consumers, patients, private sector and media
- Showcase transnational organized IP crime success stories as case studies in public awareness programmes, training materials and on the INTERPOL IP crime website

Links between IP Crime and the Financing of Terrorist Activities

Many terrorist groups engage in a variety of organized crimes to fund their activities.

As terrorist groups tend to act in similar ways to transnational organized crime groups, it is important to carefully monitor how their activities evolve.

There is general agreement that IP crime is a high-profit, low-risk crime, which inevitably motivates criminals to engage in this type of activity.

It is clear paramilitary terrorist organizations have traded in counterfeit and pirated goods to maintain their organizations and fund their activities. In light of this,

INTERPOL remains concerned about the possibility that some other terrorist groups would seize the opportunity to finance their activities through IP crime.

It is an issue that needs to be carefully monitored, and evidence of terrorist groups actually engaging in IP crime must be collected in a systematic fashion, if and when it surfaces.

IIPCAG

The current members of INTERPOL's Intellectual Property Crime Action Group IIPCAG are:

Law Enforcement:

- An Garda Siochana, Ireland
- Department of Public Security, Peoples Republic of China
- Europol
- Guarda Civil, Spain
- National Board of Customs, Finland
- National Police of Belgium
- Police Nationale of France
- Polizia Nazionale, Italy
- Policía Nacional, Mexico
- Police Service of Northern Ireland
- Policía Nacional, Spain
- Public Prosecutor for Serious Economic Crime , Denmark
- Royal Canadian Mounted Police
- United States Federal Bureau of Investigation
- United States Immigration & Customs Enforcement

Intergovernmental Agencies:

- World Customs Organization
- World Intellectual Property Organization
- Industry Groups and IPR Protection Entities:
- Coalition for Intellectual Property Rights
- Global Anti-Counterfeiting Group
- International Chamber of Commerce, BASCAP
- International Federation of the Phonographic Industries
- International Trademark Association
- Mexican Institute of Industrial Property
- Motion Picture Association
- Pharmaceutical Security Institute
- PhRMA
- Union des Fabricants
- United Kingdom Intellectual Property Office
- US Chamber of Commerce, Coalition Against Counterfeiting and Piracy

Companies:

- Microsoft Corporation
- Procter & Gamble
- Underwriters Laboratories

INTERPOL is interested in cooperating with law enforcement authorities, the public and private sectors in the fight against transnational organized IP crime.

SIGNIFICANT CASES

INTERPOL facilitates and coordinates regional law enforcement interventions in transnational and organized Intellectual Property (IP) crime throughout the world. Partnership action with national police and customs agencies supported by affected private sector entities has led to hundreds of suspects being arrested and millions of dollars worth of counterfeit and pirated goods being seized worldwide. It has also led to the identification and disruption of criminal groups producing counterfeit products on an industrialized scale.

Operation Jupiter

Intellectual property (IP) crime is a generic term used to describe a wide range of counterfeiting and piracy offences. INTERPOL contributes actively to the collective effort to combat transnational and organized intellectual property crime by facilitating and supporting cross-border operational partnerships. Examples of these efforts include Operation Jupiter, a project set up to target IP criminal activities in specific regions.

Operation Jupiter - South America focuses on enhancing partnership and prevention in the tri-border area of South America - Argentina, Brazil and Paraguay. Organized crime groups involved in IP crime typically engage in cross border activities, and the tri-border area represents a particularly challenging environment for law enforcement.

Further to the success of the different Operation Jupiter actions in South America, it is now being expanded to other INTERPOL regions, with the hope of wider cross-industry support for the initiative. While the INTERPOL General Secretariat co-ordinates action and operations, actual interventions, arrests and seizures are performed by national police and customs agencies in participating countries.

Initial Pilot Operation

A planning meeting hosted by the INTERPOL Sub-Regional Bureau for the Americas and the Argentine police was held in Buenos Aires to initialize the pilot operation. Of particular importance was the fact that representatives from the pharmaceutical, recording, motion picture and tobacco industries also took part in addition to the heads of National Central Bureaus (NCBs) from the three participating countries.

A total of twelve targets were identified, including significant counterfeiting plants and distribution centers.

Interventions took place over a four month period and resulted in significant and tangible successes. This further illustrates the value of different industry sectors sharing information and working with INTERPOL and national police forces to combat common problems.

The results of Operation Jupiter-South America were reported to the Latin America Regional Forum co-hosted by the government of Brazil and INTERPOL which took place in Rio de Janeiro shortly afterwards.

Operation Jupiter-South America I

Operation Jupiter-South America I proved that INTERPOL can act as a catalyst for action and secure the support of national police and, in partnership with the World Customs Organization (WCO), for combined enforcement action.

The INTERPOL Intellectual Property Crime Unit acknowledges the support of the national police forces and customs authorities of Argentina, Brazil and Paraguay for their outstanding contribution to the success of Operation Jupiter-South America I.

Operation Jupiter-South America I was launched with

the support and participation of the national police forces of Argentina, Brazil and Paraguay. Brazilian customs also joined the operation, together with representatives from pharmaceutical, recording, motion picture and tobacco cross-industry representative bodies.

This was the first time four different industry sectors joined together with representatives of federal police and customs agencies from the three countries to combat IP crime. There were immediate benefits for participating industry sectors. These included identification of common expertise, crime prevention measures, investigation methodologies and good practice.

During the operation, the International Federation for the Recording Industries (IFPI) worked with the federal authorities in Argentina, Brazil and Paraguay and was able to file a total of 14 complaints with supporting evidence and five individuals were arrested. Two of the arrests involved Taiwanese nationals with suspected links to organized crime.

In Brazil, customs authorities made 36 seizures and detained 79 suspects for smuggling and counterfeiting offences. The estimated value of the seized contraband/ counterfeit goods was approximately 6.2 million reais (US$3.5 million). Of the 36 seizures, three were specific anti-counterfeiting operations which resulted in 29 arrests and seizures estimated at 747,000 reais.

On the Paraguay-Brazil border customs officials seized 2.24 million blank CDs, an increase of 80 per cent from previous levels. The Federal Highway Police also routinely seized bus and truckloads of blank CDs and DVDs in the border area destined to be used for the piracy of optical disks.

In Paraguay, there were seizures of some 8,700 cartons of counterfeit cigarettes. In the port of Asunción, as a result of information from one of the pharmaceutical companies participating in Operation Jupiter, more than five million counterfeit toothbrushes were seized.

The success of these operations were dependent upon a willingness by representatives of participating industries to engage in the frank exchange of information with their counterparts in other industry sectors for the common good. The four industry sectors involved in the operation immediately recognized the benefits of doing so and pooled their expertise most effectively.

INTERPOL is an international organization and cannot carry out these types of intervention on its own. The role of the INTERPOL Intellectual Property Crime Unit was to act as a catalyst by facilitating and coordinating activities.

It was the national law enforcement agencies who actually did the hard work, invested resources and put their people in harm's way to deliver these results.

The INTERPOL Intellectual Property Crime Unit acknowledges the support of the national police forces and customs authorities of Argentina, Brazil and Paraguay for their outstanding contribution to the success of Operation Jupiter-South America I.

Operation Jupiter - South America II

A conservative estimate of the total potential retail value of contraband and counterfeit products seized by the five participating countries during this operation is in excess of US$35 million. 54 searches were carried out in the greater Buenos Aires area resulting in the disruption of counterfeit human and animal medicine product manufacturing.

Operation Fireball, which focused on the apparent flow of counterfeit cigarettes from Paraguay to Brazil, resulted in 25 police operations in 11 Brazilian States. 360,000 blank

CDs concealed as toy products and smuggled into Paraguay via Montevideo were seized. Uruguayan police arrested one organized criminal wanted by the Brazilian authorities in connection with Operation Fireball and the subject of an INTERPOL Red Notice.

The second Operation Jupiter - South America was carried out shortly after the first, this time with the additional participation of Chile and Uruguay.

The operation was facilitated and coordinated by INTERPOL's IP Crime Unit and the INTERPOL Sub-regional Bureau for South America with the assistance of the General Secretariats Directorate for Sub-regional Bureau Management (RBM).

Three planning meetings chaired by INTERPOL and attended by representatives from participating industries and IP crime affected industry sectors were held in Buenos Aires and Iquique prior to launching this second operation. It should be noted that the role of INTERPOL was to act as a catalyst for action and coordinate the operation. Actual interventions, arrests and seizures were carried out by police and customs agencies in participating countries.

The additional participation of Chile and Uruguay meant the flow of suspected counterfeit goods in and out of the ports of Iquique in Chile and Montevideo in Uruguay was monitored. Intelligence arising from this surveillance was used to inform the operational deployments of police and customs officers in the tri-border area.

A feature of the second operation compared to the first was the increased involvement of customs authorities in each of the countries. In some instances prosecutors also contributed to the planning process. There were also more industry sectors participating in the operation, with representatives from luxury goods manufacturers joining the original four industry sectors (Pharmaceutical, recording, motion picture and tobacco industries).

The intelligence flow before, during and after the operation was far better than previously experienced in the region. This combined with enhanced coordination by INTERPOL led to significantly improved results.

Involvement of Transnational Organized Crime Groups

An analysis of the counterfeit and pirate products seized and suspects arrested in the tri-border region during Operation Jupiter - South America II clearly illustrated the nature and extent of transnational organized criminal involvement in these offences.

A common denominator is that foreign nationals and nationals of Middle Eastern and Asian countries were well represented in these criminal conspiracies. Analysis indicated that typically transnational organized criminals of Arab, Indian and Pakistani origin have a controlling influence in informatics. Typically transnational organized criminals of Chinese origin have a controlling influence in CD/DVD pirate manufacturing and distribution as well as sports clothes and luxury goods.

Results

It is often difficult to quantify the value of seized counterfeit and pirate products. However, a conservative estimate of the total potential retail value of contraband and counterfeit products seized by the five participating countries during this operation is in excess of US$35 Million.

The type of counterfeit and pirate goods seized varied from country to country. They included CDs; chemicals; cigarettes; clothing; computer hardware and software; DVDs; domestic electrical goods; electronics; fabrics; medical products including counterfeit body building products; medicines; shoes; textiles; toys and vehicle parts.

A total of nine illicit CD/DVD manufacturing plants producing pirated products on an industrialized scale were identified and closed during the course of the operation by police and customs officials working in partnership with the recording and motion picture industries.

Many of the seized product types including counterfeit domestic electrical goods; medical products including body building products; medicines; toys; and, vehicle parts had the potential to affect the health and safety of consumers.

Apart from counterfeit and pirate goods other illicit commodities were seized - including more than 3,000 rounds of different caliber ammunition; 1600 kilos of cannabis; and, 3.2 kilos of cocaine.

Highlights of each country's results arising from police and customs interventions, and reported to INTERPOL are shown below.

Argentina

- Police and customs authorities seized counterfeit and pirate products valued at in excess of US$8.5 Million
- Product included CDs; chemicals; cigarettes; clothing; computer hardware and software; DVDs; domestic electrical goods; electronics; fabrics; medical products; medicines; shoes; textiles; toys; and vehicle parts.
- a transnational organized crime gang that sold counterfeit body building products through the Internet was identified and dismantled
- 54 searches carried out in the greater Buenos Aires area resulting in the disruption of the manufacture of counterfeit human and animal medicines

- as a result of investigative work during Operation Jupiter, 77 tons of blank CDs and DVDs imported from Taiwan and to be used to produce pirated product were seized

Brazil

- Police and customs authorities seized counterfeit and pirated products valued at in excess of US$8 Million
- Products included CDs; cigarettes; clothing; computer hardware and software; DVDs; domestic electrical goods; electronics; fabrics; medical products; medicines; shoes; textiles; and, toys
- Operation Fireball, which focused on the apparent flow of counterfeit cigarettes from Paraguay to Brazil, was carried out resulting in 25 police operations in 11 Brazilian States. It was established the cigarettes were actually manufactured in Brazil and were the subject of tax evasion. Cigarettes valued at US$5.3 Million seized, 90 suspects arrested and 70 vehicles confiscated. US$1 Million in cash recovered and six INTERPOL Red Notices issued. Operation Fireball remains the single biggest anti-cigarette counterfeiting/contraband operation in Brazilian history
- 50 vehicles seized containing a total of 130 cartons of counterfeit products and four boxes of ammunition
- 1108 rounds of ammunition seized hidden in a consignment of counterfeit cigarettes, clothing and toys
- 1.8 kilos of crack cocaine seized
- 1.5 kilos of cocaine seized
- 1550 rounds of ammunition seized

- 265 cartons of counterfeit cigarettes, electronic equipment, medicines valued at US$53,000 seized. Hidden in the consignment were 1400 kilos of cannabis

Chile

- Products included CDs; clothing; computer hardware and software; DVDs; domestic electrical goods; electronics; fabrics; textiles; and toys
- 12,888 counterfeit towels and 720 rolls of fabric valued at US$121,722 seized
- 6,434 pirate CDs and DVDs together with seven CD/ DVD burner equipment and 6,500 pieces of cover art work seized
- 2,194 pirate CDs and DVDs together with five CD/ DVD burner equipment and 3,000 pieces of cover art work seized
- 3,000 counterfeit toys seized
- 19 CD/DVD burner equipment together with 19 computers, 12 printers, 15 games consoles and 9,500 pieces of art work seized

Paraguay

- Products included CDs; cigarettes; clothing; computer hardware and software; DVDs; domestic electrical goods; electronics; shoes; textiles; and toys
- 3112 pirate CDs and DVDs together with 64 CD/DVD burner equipment; six burner coordinating units and cover art work seized
- 46 CD/DVD burner equipment together with six burner coordinating units seized
- Counterfeit cigarettes together valued at US$463,207 seized

- 111 CD/DVD burner equipment together with eight coordinating burner units, 14 computers, 12,846 blank CDs with cover art work seized
- 1344 units of counterfeit toothpaste valued at US$3,500
- 41,076 counterfeit Spider man toys seized
- 35,000 counterfeit Chanel sunglasses valued at US$1.32 Million seized
- 360,000 blank CDs secreted under toy products and smuggled into Paraguay via Montevideo seized
- 141,247 counterfeit cell phone accessories including batteries seized
- 450 counterfeit toys and 536 counterfeit dolls seized
- the Paraguayan police arrested two organized criminals wanted by the Brazilian authorities in connection with Operation Fireball
- 29 CD/DVD burner equipment together with five burner coordinating units, one photocopy machine, 3197 DVDs and 765 printed cover art work seized
- 144,000 counterfeit cell phone accessories including batteries seized

Uruguay

- Police and customs authorities seized counterfeit and pirate product valued at in excess of US$8 Million
- Products included CDs; cigarettes; clothing; computer hardware and software; DVDs; domestic electrical goods; electronics; shoes; and textiles
- Uruguayan police arrested one organized criminal wanted by the Brazilian authorities in connection

with Operation Fireball and the subject of an INTERPOL Red Notice

- three CD/DVD burner equipment together with 18 computers, four scanners and eight printers seized
- 29,000 pieces of counterfeit luxury brand clothing seized
- as a result of investigative work during Operation Jupiter a Uruguayan suspect for copyright infringement using the Internet to systematically distribute infringed publications in Argentina, Brazil and Uruguay arrested

Conclusion

Operation Jupiter - South America II confirmed INTERPOL is uniquely positioned to facilitate and coordinate collective law enforcement interventions in the counterfeit and pirate activities of transnational organized criminals.

It reconfirmed the willingness of INTERPOL member countries and their INTERPOL National Central Bureaus to work with the INTERPOL IP Crime Unit, INTERPOL Sub-regional Bureau for South America and INTERPOL Sub-regional Bureau Management Directorate (RBM) to tackle and resolve collective problems.

It illustrates the benefits police, customs, prosecutors and representatives of IP crime affected industries derive from working together in partnership to combat transnational organized IP crime.

INTERPOL recognizes the contribution made by the police and customs authorities in Argentina, Brazil, Chile, Paraguay and Uruguay before, during and after Operation Jupiter II. Without their enthusiastic cooperation, interest and support the benefits derived by all participants would not have materialized.

The INTERPOL IP Crime Unit would especially like to thank the Head and staff of the INTERPOL Sub-regional Bureau for South America for their efforts and regional leadership role in bringing this operation to fruition.

THE BEATLES CASE

The International Federation for the Phonographic Industry (IFPI) started an investigation into the theft of a number of original unreleased music recordings by The Beatles.

These recordings were made in 1969 and subsequent versions of the work were released on the album 'Let It Be'. These priceless pieces of musical heritage were stolen when the record company relocated to new offices.

The IFPI, in partnership with the City of London Police in the United Kingdom, established that some of the stolen items had surfaced in Luxembourg, where they had been pirated.

The search warrant executed by the Luxembourg authorities also recovered pirated copies of the stolen Beatles recordings. As a result of further investigations, police were able to establish that the person who stole the original Beatles recordings was an engineer working in the studio where they were stored.

He was arrested and admitted to having kept a copy for himself and sold the original recordings to two Dutch nationals for £50,000.

An undercover operation was mounted by the City of London Police in an effort to recover the original recordings, and police were able to arrange a meeting with the suspects with an offer to buy the original recordings for £250,000.

The meeting was scheduled to take place two weeks later in the Netherlands. Because of the urgency of the case, the

City of London Police sought the assistance of the INTERPOL IP Crime Unit, which used I-24/7, the organization's secure global police communications system, and personal contacts to expedite the request to Dutch authorities for the authority and necessary assistance to undertake the undercover operation in the Netherlands.

A series of raids was carried out in the Netherlands and United Kingdom. Five hundred original reel-to-reel tapes featuring the Beatles music were seized and six suspects arrested for theft and handling stolen goods

Cross-border CD Counterfeiting Activity

The International Federation for the Phonographic Industry (IFPI) asked INTERPOL's IP Crime Unit for assistance in an ongoing investigation into cross-border and organised CD counterfeiting activity centered on Luxembourg, Austria and the UK.

IFPI investigations had established the identity and location of distribution centers in the three countries, but the principal suspect was believed to be operating on a global scale.

The INTERPOL IP Crime Unit used I-24/7 and established direct contacts to obtain the cooperation of British, Austrian and Luxembourg law enforcement officers. The Austrian authorities assisted the IP Crime Unit by deploying investigative resources to identify the location of a second building which was found to be another business address of the principal suspect.

The INTERPOL IP Crime Unit then coordinated the activities of the Luxembourg, Austrian and British authorities to carry out simultaneous raids in all three countries. These raids led to the seizure of 1.5 million counterfeit CDs. This remains the biggest single seizure in Europe and had significant implications for the Beatles case.

Belgrade Case - Counterfeit CDs

The International Federation for the Phonographic Industry (IFPI) provided INTERPOL with information about a plant in Belgrade that produced counterfeit CDs. The equipment used in the manufacturing plant was acquired from another operation in Italy.

The source plant in Italy was also responsible for supplying similar equipment to other counterfeiting operations in Bulgaria and Russia. These connections were established by forensic analysis of the counterfeit CDs manufactured using these apparently unconnected pieces of equipment.

As a result, the industry was able to prove the extent of the music piracy activity and link the Belgrade plant in Serbia to the investigations in Bulgaria and Russia.

INTERPOL's IP Crime Unit was contacted, and through I-24/7 and direct contacts, it was confirmed to Serbian authorities that the Belgrade plant was part of an international organized crime operation. As a result of the intervention by INTERPOL, police in Belgrade initiated an investigation and raided the plant. A total of 750,000 counterfeit CDs were seized.

Child Abuse Investigation

There are also instances where partnerships between INTERPOL and industries affected by IP crime have led to the successful conclusion of police investigations into a wide range of serious criminal offences.

INTERPOL crime intelligence officers responsible for the investigation of child pornography asked IIPCAG for assistance. During the course of an international cross-border investigation into child abuse images posted on the Internet, the investigating officer was able to obtain images of two unidentified suspects. A bottle of shampoo appeared in the background of one of the images, but the brand could not be ascertained. This was the only available lead to help investigators identify the location of the offence.

The image was circulated to industry and law enforcement members of the IIPCAG by the IP Crime Unit in an attempt to identify the brand. Shortly thereafter, representatives of Procter & Gamble provided information that indicated the product was manufactured in Germany. As a direct result of this information, investigators were able to focus their enquiries on Germany. One of the suspects was arrested and charged with child pornography offences by German authorities.

COUNTERFEIT CURRENCY

The crime of counterfeiting currency is as old as money itself. In the past, nations had used counterfeiting as a means of warfare, such as in the War Between the States in the USA in the mid-1800s and the Bernhard Operation in Europe during the Second World War. The idea was to overflow the enemy's economy with fake banknotes, so that the real value of the said money was reduced; therefore, attacking the economy and general welfare of a society.

Today, the crime of counterfeiting continues to present a potential danger to national economies and financial losses to consumers. Recent developments in photographic and computer technology, as well as printing devices, have made the production of counterfeit money relatively easy, thereby increasing the potential threat.

Cooperation, Communication, and Contacts

The INTERPOL Counterfeits and Security Documents Branch (CSDB) is responsible for establishing programs that provide forensic support, operational assistance, and technical databases in order to assist the 186 member countries of INTERPOL regarding counterfeit currency. With this responsibility, INTERPOL CSDB continuously assesses existing measures, with the goal of implementing new ones that may provide an "added value" to the international community in addressing counterfeit currency on a global scale.

The major challenge to protect currencies from counterfeiters has increasingly become more dependant on partnerships between law enforcement agencies, financial institutions and central banks, as well as with the security printing industry and high-grade supplier's community.

These partnerships bridge geographic, jurisdictional, cultural and organizational divisions, which were once impediments toward providing comprehensive and co-coordinated solutions for combating modern financial crimes.

Therefore, INTERPOL, through its Counterfeits and Security Documents Branch (CSDB), recognizes and fosters cooperation with other official law enforcement entities, such as the United States Secret Service (USSS) and Europol; as well as with international organizations and central banks, such as the European Anti-Fraud Office (OLAF), European Central Bank (ECB), the US Federal Reserve Bank (FRB), and the Central Bank Counterfeit Deterrence Group (CBCDG); and with innovative leaders in private industry.

The INTERPOL CSDB philosophy is that throughpartnerships --- and increased cooperation, communication, and contacts --- we can better serve the needs of the community and reduce duplicity of effort, while combating this particular crime.

INTERPOL Assistance in the Prevention of Currency Counterfeiting

Since the 1929 Geneva Convention, which recognized

the ICPO-General Secretariat as the International Central Office for the suppression of counterfeit currency, INTERPOL member countries have been able to call upon the General Secretariat for the following services:

- Classifying, analyzing and storing genuine currency specimens and counterfeit banknotes
- Circulating analytical reports among INTERPOL member countries
- Determining whether suspect specimens are genuine or counterfeit
- Allocating international indicatives to newly discovered counterfeits, (except for USD and Euro)
- Publishing descriptions of new counterfeit banknotes
- Preparing and circulating tables of statistics on worldwide counterfeit currency trends
- Organizing and/or participating in international counterfeit currency training courses, seminars and conferences, in order to stay abreast of latest technologies and to share best practices.

'Public-Private' Outreach

In an effort to address new trends in the area counterfeit currency --- as well as encourage the international spirit of cooperation --- representatives of INTERPOL CSDB routinely participate in public events and private training seminars, with our partners from law enforcement, the central banking community, and the security printing industry.

CSDB Web-Based Tools

In addition to our 'Public-Private' outreach activities, representatives of INTERPOL CSDB are also continuously developing web-based tools in order to address currency concerns within the 186 members of the ICPO community. Over recent years, CSDB has developed the following web-based tools, which are available via the INTERPOL secure communication network, I-24/7:

- Currency Bulletins - A publication posted monthly with the assistance of our ICPO members and their respective national central banks, which provides current trends and specific details about the genuine currencies within the ICPO community.
- Currency List - An electronic listing of all 186 members of the ICPO community with direct links to the respective national central banks. (Also available on the public site).
- Early Warning Messages - A monthly publication, posted in conjunction with Europol and the ECB in order to provide relevant trends involving counterfeit Euro currency.
- Counterfeit Alerts - A posting of newly discovered counterfeit currencies --- Non-US Dollar and non-Euro --- along with a detailed forensic analysis to warn specific region of the ICPO community about the potential impact.
- Counterfeit Currency List (CCL) - To disseminate information on known counterfeits regarding the other currencies of the ICPO community --- non-US Dollar and non-Euro --- which have also exhibited a global impact as well as global circulation.
- CSDB News - A web-based product to inform the ICPO community about recent activities of the CSDB Counterfeit Currency Team. (As mentioned above, and also available on the public site).

2

INFORMATION TECHNOLOGY CRIME

Interpol has actively been involved for a number of years in combating Information Technology Crime. Rather than 're-inventing the wheel', the Interpol General Secretariat has harnessed the expertise of its members in the field of Information Technology Crime (ITC) through the vehicle of a 'working party' or a group of experts.

In this instance, the working party consists of the heads or experienced members of national computer crime units. These working parties have been designed to reflect regional expertise and exist in Europe, Asia, the Americas and in Africa. All working parties are in different stages of development. It should be noted that the work done by the working parties is not Interpol's only contribution to combating ITC, but it certainly represents the most noteworthy contribution to date.

Regional Working Parties

- European Working Party on Information Technology Crime
- African Regional Working Party on Information Technology Crime
- Asia - South Pacific Working Party on Information Technology Crime

- Latin America Working Party on Information Technology Crime

European Working Party on Information Technology Crime

Formed in 1990, it meets three times a year. In 2005 the Interpol General Secretariat will host 3 meetings of the working party. It is currently represented by members from Austria, Belgium, Denmark, Finland, France, Germany, Italy, Netherlands, Norway, Portugal, Sweden, Switzerland, Spain, and United Kingdom.

48th Meeting of Interpol Working Party on IT Crime - Europe: 16 - 18. January 2007

49th Meeting of Interpol Working Party on IT Crime - Europe: 22 - 24 May 2007

50th Meeting of Interpol Working Party on IT Crime - Europe: 2 - 5 October 2007

Amongst its many achievements are:

the compilation of the Computer Crime Manual, now called Information Technology Crime Investigation Manual (ITCIM), a best practise guide for the experienced investigator, which is continually updated; in order to be more practical (in terms of its volume) and cost efficient, the manual has been made available on CD; an updated version of the CD is currently under production. The content of the Computer Crime Manual is also being converted into HTML format, and is digitally available via Interpol's restricted website; Amongst many others the ' following projects are available for Law Enforcement only in the new ITCIM:

Electronic Means of Payment: this project deals with the various methods and tools used for secure electronic transactions.

Manipulation of Public Communications Network: this project describes different modi operandi and case studies concerning telecom fraud and hacking schemes.

Criminal Threats against e-commerce: The question of secure transactions along with the increasing number of e-commerce transactions has become an important issue in the combating of Information Technology Crime. Here too a project team with special skills has been mandated to research this subject and to devise protocols which will allow law enforcement to deal effectively with this problem, as well as to advise potential users on precautionary - and safety measures.

Tools and Techniques 2: This project group was mandated with the aim of providing law enforcement with an in-depth overview of the tools and techniques utilised for the investigation of Information Technology Crime and to provide an extensive list of these and the value of their application at the conclusion of the project.

Internet Investigations 2-4: The aim of this projects is to develop advanced investigation manual, based on practical experiences. It represents additional aid, besides the already existing project 'Internet misuse and elementary Internet investigations'. The advanced investigation manual is addressed specifically to investigators working on Internet related crime.

Wireless Technology: Threat assessment of evolving technologies:

- numerous training courses in order to share its expertise with other members; these are not only extremely cost efficient (and presented by law enforcement experts for the benefit of law enforcement), but are designed to aim at different levels of expertise and subject areas, ranging from introductory courses to courses specialising in Internet investigations. For 2006 the following courses are currently scheduled:

Internet Investigations course, 4 - 8 June 2007 Tampere/Finland

- These training courses are being held in English only and are self-funded. The participation fees for accommodation, meals and course lectures amount to EUR 850 for each course. Transport costs to the course location are to be born by the participants. The courses are open to law enforcement members. For inscription procedures and further information please contact your NCB;
- a rapid information exchange system which essentially consists of two elements: an international 24-hour response system, the National Central Reference Points (listing responsible experts within more than 100 countries currently listed- this is now being expanded and has been endorsed by the High Tech Crime Sub-group of the G8) and a formatted computer crime message format (to ensure that all the essential information is transmitted);
- The WP also recognised the necessity to complement its expertise with additional outside expertise; in order to not make the WP too cumbersome, this additional expertise (which is not restricted to law enforcement) was incorporated into so-called 'project groups' and is selected by studying the curriculum vitae received in response to a general invitation to European member countries; these project groups are specific task motivated groups led by WP members who within the framework of a specific set period have to complete their project (the meetings are merely used to coordinate and streamline the efforts of the

individuals, the real work is done on their own time- this has proven to be a very successful and time efficient method).

Future

The EWPITC agreed to prioritise the following projects:

Training: Collection of existing training material, internationalize it and create training packages for global LE use; a picture of needed IT Crime investigation courses will be produced to make sure that all needed areas are covered; aims and objectives for every training module will be defined.

BotNets and Malicious Codes: The benefit of this project will be that law enforcement agencies worldwide will be better able to investigate botnets and malicious code. The project will also aim to facilitate an operational cooperation project of European BotNet investigators to share intelligence and best practices, in coordination with work being done on this by the General Secretariat.

Mobile Phone Forensics: The objectives for this project are to compile a best practice guide based on different national initiatives on describing the current forensic tools for mobile phones.

Voice over IP - VoIP: The purpose of the project is to give a description of the Voice over IP (VoIP) technology, available services related to VoIP and how to investigate criminal cases where VoIP is involved. The description should cover different tools and techniques on analysing computers and other equipment used to communicate through VoIP services.

Tools and Techniques 3: The aim of this project is to write a document describing the current forensic tools for IT Investigations (Protocol) in particular for:

- device /media imaging ('bit stream' copy)
- device/media write protection (software and hardware methods)
- image (and/or file system) analysis.
- revision of the Information Technology Crime Investigation Manual.

AFRICAN REGIONAL WORKING PARTY ON INFORMATION TECHNOLOGY CRIME

The current chairman is Mr Beaunard Grobler from the Cyber Crime Unit of the South African Police Service, Vice-Chairmen are Mr. Mboya Tom Gerald (Kenya), and Mr Kassala Samso (Tanzania).

The Technical Advisor to the Working Party is Professor Dana van der Merwe from the Department of Criminal and Procedural Law of the University of South Africa in Pretoria. The group agreed unanimously on following objectives for the African Working Party on Information Technology Crime:

- Developing and making expertise available for combating IT crime in the region and inter-regional
- Develop and enhance partnerships with organizations, which deal with IT crime
- Establish, coordinate and promote the use of best practices in investigation and prevention of IT crime
- Increase information flow within the regional Computer Crime units
- Promotion of operating procedures standardization in the African region

The group agreed unanimously on following project for the Interpol Working Party on Information Technology Crime-Africa:

To run an awareness program for the top management level for African countries and regional police organisations and to start targeting all African countries with information on IT Crime on a regular basis. The Heads of CIDs should be invited to the next meeting of the group to formulate a plan of action to deplo. Cyber Crime Units.

Esther KGHOLE (SAPS) was unanimously nominated as project Co-Ordinator.

As activities of IPSG for combating High-Tech Crime in Asia-South Pacific (ASP), IPSG annually holds 2 Meetings and 2 Training Workshops for ASP member countries.

Interpol Working Party on IT Crime - ASP (ASPWP)

Objectives: Interpol Working Party on IT Crimes - Asia South Pacific region was established in 1997 and annual meeting is being held.

The aims of this Working Party are:

- Cooperation, sharing of knowledge and practical experience
- Promotion of standardization of methods such as Investigation method, training method and so on
- And establish good practice guidelines

and practical activities are

- To share significant expertise
- To share the current crime scenes
- To establish new projects

Nowadays, 4 projects are on going on this Working Party.

- Intelligent Scoping Project (Leader: IPSG): to measure and scope the current situation on IT crime and the current law enforcement initiative against such crime.

- Case Information Sharing Project (Leader: Korea): to share the experience of IT Crime investigations and study from the investigation strategies from other cases
- Training Project: (Leader: Hong Kong): to create/ update training manuals and provide training to member countries
- Computer Forensic Project (Leader: Japan): to share the experience of computer forensics for various types of digital devices

Previous ASPWP:

- 1st meeting in Melbourne, Australia from 17 to 19 February 1997
- 2nd meeting in New Delhi, India from 20 to 22 November 2000
- 3rd meeting in Hong Kong, China from 26 to 28 November 2001
- 4th meeting in Seoul, Korea from 17-18 October 2002
- 5th meeting in Shanghai, China
- 6th meeting in Bangkok, Thailand from 15 to 17 December 2004
- 7th meeting in Tokyo, Japan from 28-30 September 2005
- 8th meeting in Hong Kong, China from 19-21 December 2006

Future ASPWP:

- 9th meeting in Bali, Indonesia, November 2007

Minute of Last ASPWP: The 8th Interpol Working Party on IT Crime for Asia and South Pacific was held from 19 to 21 December in Hong Kong, China. 34 participants from 11 countries/regions, Australia, Bangladesh, China, Hong Kong China, India, Indonesia, Iran, Japan, Korea, Malaysia, Pakistan, Singapore and Sri Lanka attended the Working Party thanks to the Co-Host of Hong Kong Police Force.

In this Working Party, after 2 Vice Chairperson's election, participants discussed about 4 Projects such as Intelligence Scoping Project, Case Information Project, Training Project and Computer Forensic Project. Also guest speakers from Microsoft made presentations.

Participants could share the knowledge on the field of High-Tech facilitated Criminality and agreed to update their country reports by the end of next January and to continue to keep in touch with each other by updating the list of NCRP consequently.

Also in line with the initiative of the Train-the-Trainer Workshop organized by Interpol, trainers and experts in ASP region gathered at the CTINS server which is controlled by Japanese National Police Agency and continued to discuss about creating the materials of forensic course and updating the IT crime investigation course.

As for the Projects, participant agreed to begin the new projects such as 'Investigative Reference Project' for gathering the legislation information to mutual assistance on the field of investigation faster, '3G Project' to share the knowledge about the 3 Giga Hz technology and 'Mobile Phone Forensic Project' to find the method to do forensic for various types of Mobile Phone.

Released Documents:

8th ASPWP: SMinute of 8th ASPWP meeting in Hong Kong, China (02/Jan/2007).

Intelligence Scoping Project Report: Scoping and Responding to Information Technology Crime, Asia and South

Pacific Interpol Information Technology Crime Investigation and Training Seminar (SEMINAR)

Objectives: Seminar is mainly for the TECHNICAL EXPERTS on the field of combating High-tech crime investigation and digital forensics.

They gather and discuss about new and essential technical issues. SEMINAR is targeted on the 3 areas in line with the projects of ASPWP.

There are:

- IT Crime Investigation
- IT Crime Training
- Computer forensics

and as an important task, SEMINAR is recommended to make reports and feed them back to ASPWP.

Previous Seminars:

- 1st SEMINAR in Hong Kong, China from 6-8 October 2003
- 2nd SEMINAR in Seoul, Korea from 19-21 July 2004
- 3rd SEMINAR in Xi'an, China from 17 to 19 May 2005
- 4th SEMINAR in Tokyo, Japan from 27 to 29 September 2006
- 5th SEMINAR in Tokyo, Japan from 2-4 October 2007

Minute of Last Seminar: 5th INTERPOL Information Technology Crime Investigation and Training Seminar was held from 2 to 4 October in Tokyo, Japan. 28 participants from 13 countries/jurisdictions attended this Seminar and shared lot of technical-oriented information relating to IT Crime Investigation, methods and materials for training investigators and digital forensics to combat High-Tech Facilitated Criminality.

The participants, in particular, discussed about BOTNETS, P2P Networks, Information Leakage, Phishing Scam, Data Analysis of e-mails, windows vista and hands-on Forensic examinations. Also teaching materials of Training Workshop on Investigation and Forensic were discussed to be updated. All summaries are now available to see by click above 5th SEMINAR in Tokyo, Japan from 2-4 October 2007.

Train-the-Trainer Workshop on Information Technology Crime Investigation for ASP (TTI)

Objectives: In October 2003, 5th Interpol Asia and South Pacific Working party on Information Technology crime agreed to hold the 'Train-the-Trainer Workshop on Information Technology Crime Investigation' annually, in order to provide a training opportunity cheaply to increase the number of Information Technology Crime investigators in Asia and South Pacific region.

Previous TTI:

- 1st TTI in Seoul, Korea from 8 to 12 November 2004
- 2nd TTI in American Samoa, USA from 13 to 17 June 2005
- 3rd TTI in Tokyo, Japan from 9 to 13 January 2006
- 4th TTI in Melbourne, Australia from 13 to 17 November 2006

Future TTI:

- 5th TTI in Seoul, Korea June 2007

Minute of Last TTI: The fourth Train-the-Trainer Workshop on Information Technology Crime Investigation for Asia and South Pacific was held from 13 to 17 November, which was the second training workshop held in South Pacific.

21 participants from American Samoa USA, Australia, China, Fiji, Myanmar, Philippines and Timor LESTE joined the workshop and 5 trainers from Australia, Hong Kong China and Korea lectured to them. Trainees were taught about IT Crime investigation knowledge mainly and in additional digital forensics which is essential knowledge for investigators.

According to the feedback from the participants, every participant said that this workshop was useful for their development of national training programs and most of them said the materials had good quality.

Released Documents:

4th TTI: Timetable of 4th TTI in Melbourne, Australia (30/Nov/2006)

4th TTI: Minute of 4th TTI in Melbourne, Australia (29/Dec/2006)

4th TTI: Contents of 4th TTI in Melbourne, Australia (29/Dec/2006)

4th TTI: Evaluation Results, Usefulness of 4th TTI in Melbourne, Australia (29/Dec/2006)

4th TTI: Evaluation Results, Delivery of 4th TTI in Melbourne, Australia (29/Dec/2006)

Note: Teaching Material of TTI (PowerPoint Presentation) is now compiled on CD. You may contact IPSG - FHT High-Tech team to obtain it.

Train-the-Trainer Workshop on Computer Forensic for ASP (TTF)

Objectives: On the basis of the success of Investigation Training Workshop, 7th Interpol Working Party on IT Crime-ASP in Japan agreed to hold 'Train-the-Trainer Workshop on Computer Forensics' annually, in order to provide a training opportunity cheaply to increase the number of the officers who is in charge of digital forensics in Asia and South Pacific region, as well as TTI.

Previous TTF: None

Future TTF: 1st TTF in Tokyo, Japan from 22 to 26 January 2007

Formed in 2005, as activities of IPSG for combating High-Tech Crime in Latin America IPSG annually holds 1 or 2 Meetings for member countries.

Delegates from Argentina, Brazil, Bolivia, Chile, Colombia, Costa Rica, Cuba, Dominican Republic, Ecuador, El Salvador, Mexico, Nicaragua, Panama, Peru, Spain, Uruguay and Venezuela have participated in these Working Parties since the first meeting in November 2005.

The current chairman is Mr Jaime Edgardo Jara Retamal (Chile), First Vice-Chairmen is Mr Fredy Bautista García (Colombia) and Second Vice-President is Mr Juan Salom Clotet (Spain).

Objectives: The aims of this Working Party are:

- Cooperation, sharing of knowledge and practical experience among INTERPOL member countries and other International Organizations dealing with High-Tech Crime.
- Promotion of standardization of methods and working proceedings to combat efficiently cyber crime.
- Establishment of good practice guidelines

And practical activities are:

- To coordinate with the rest of INTERPOL working parties on IT Crime.
- To promote international police cooperation among Latin American countries.

- Expertise Sharing: to share the experience of IT Crime investigations.
- Creation and supervision of Working Sub-Groups responsible for covering the necessities of the specialized units dealing with high-tech crime in Latin America.
- Analysis of criminal trends and investigation methods.

Previous LAWPITC:

- 1st meeting in San Salvador, El Salvador from 28 to 30 November 2005
- 2nd meeting in Buenos Aires, Argentina from 15 to 17 May 2006
- 1st board meeting in Cartagena de Indias, Colombia from 25 to 29 September 2006
- 3rd meeting in Panama City, Republic of Panama from 24 to 26 January 2007
- 2nd board meeting in Bogota, Colombia from 7 to 8 June 2007

Future LAWPITC:

- 4th meeting in Chile: first half 2008 (Place and dates to be confirmed)
- 5th meeting in San Salvador: second half 2008 (Place and dates to be confirmed)

WIRELESS TECHNOLOGY

Description

As the name suggests, a wireless local area network (WLAN) is one to which a computer can be connected without wires by means of so-called 'access points' or radio stations distributed throughout a building. Each access point has a particular range and serves a maximum number of clients.

A significant characteristic of WLAN is that a user has to share an access point with several other clients. This is known as 'shared media'. Multiple computer users use the same bandwidth and can listen in on all messages which are sent to and from the access point.

In 1999, Apple was the first major hardware company to introduce a wireless system for computers and printers in offices. The transmitter/receiver was named 'Airport' and was based on the open wireless local network standard, 802.11b, originally called Wave-LAN. Since then, a local area network (LAN) based on this standard has become known as a WLAN.

Since WLAN was developed for local networks such as computers on an office floor, its maximum theoretical open-air radio range is 12 kilometres, but 50 metres is the maximum range usually achievable in offices. Data which is sent or received by a computer is transmitted at a maximum speed of 11 Mbps.

A 'hotspot' is a place where WLAN access is offered to all, either paid or free of charge. Hotspots are already common in places such as airports and hotels, and are now being deployed more widely, including in the open air.

Criminal Possibilities

Radio communication differs from wired communication because of the transmission medium. Access to data transmitted by cable is relatively simple to control. Unless very sophisticated equipment is used, data on a cable cannot be retrieved without physical access to the cable. Radio waves form the transmission medium for wireless communication. These waves are emitted in all or most directions from a transmitter. Transmitter output decreases in line with the distance from the source. The radius of effective propagation is smaller in built-up areas and is difficult to estimate.

Even though propagation can be partially controlled by the choice of antenna and transmitter output, the range of wireless communication in private networks does not stop at the wall of a building. In practice, this means that data transmitted by a company or institution using wireless communication can often be received on public property.

Four factors make today's widespread wireless computer networks based on IEEE 802.11b considerably less safe than wireless telephones:

1. The data in computer networks contain a much wider range of information than in telephone conversations.
2. Because the data is electronically available, it requires no special technology to save and filter for items of interest.
3. Networks potentially enable access to much more information. It is often possible via Wave-LAN to circumvent a company's firewall, thereby gaining unfettered access to the company's internal network.
4. While tapping wireless telephones requires sophisticated technology, the only thing that is necessary to access wireless computer networks is a widely available adaptation of the network software.

Here are some possible scenarios of unauthorised access to a private WLAN:

INTERNET

An unauthorised user could use another individual's Internet access, which would guarantee the unauthorised user a great degree of anonymity. In addition to the costs involved, all of the unauthorised user's actions on the Internet - including possible criminal offences - would appear to originate from the individual whose Internet account had been unlawfully accessed.

Monitoring Communication

An unauthorised person could monitor communication within a wireless network and possibly elsewhere within the same company's network.

Data Theft

The fact that an unauthorised user could access a network from inside means that he or she will very likely be able to read data within the network which could not otherwise be accessed from outside.

Data Manipulation

An unauthorised user could change data which has already been saved or is being transmitted.

In addition to these illicit uses of a private WLAN, a client who uses a hotspot to transmit unencrypted data opens up the possibility for criminals to monitor - and possibly even modify - that data. There are also possibilities for criminals to piggy-back on communications to get inside corporate networks.

In the Future

IEEE 802.11b, with its maximum transmission rate of 11 Mbps, is presently used in nearly all hotspots worldwide. The effective bandwidth this standard offers the user is sufficient at present for conventional applications such as the web and e-mail.

The speed of WLAN will continue to increase in the future until an equivalent to the widespread existing 802.3 100 Mbps network is available. The individual user will have more bandwidth at the hotspot and will be able to use more bandwidth-intensive applications such as voice over Internet protocol, video conferencing and video streaming.

Hotspots will spread more rapidly and become established in all areas of public life where mobile Internet access is attractive. In the future, the user will be able to receive information without delay nearly everywhere.

Since communication technologies such as UMTS and GPRS will become integrated, more and more private clients will use hotspots in the future as opposed to mainly business users today. However, it is not clear if the increased use of hotspots will be accompanied by corresponding awareness of their related security issues.

3G MOBILE PHONES

Description

Telecommunication providers are introducing a new generation of mobile telephone technology, (third generation, or 3G), which will enable increased data-handling rates. This will allow mobile telephones to offer new features such as video streaming, video conference calling, transmission of video calls, and enhanced e-mail and web-browsing capabilities.

There is considerable variety in the uptake across European countries: for example, in Italy, nearly 50% of mobile telephones are 3G units. In Japan, uptake has been even more rapid - up to 60% of units are 3G capable.

Criminal Possibilities

There is a potential criminal market in stolen units given their high unit value. 'Chipping and pinning', the reprogramming of phones and personal identification numbers, is already widely available at the street level for pre-3G phones. If this becomes possible with 3G units, it could lead to a rise in related thefts.

When units are stolen, there are issues related to the security of any sensitive data held on the units. This is a serious problem with 3G phones as they are in effect a crossover between telephones and portable computers. Data held on the units such as card or account numbers could be used to commit further fraud or theft.

The streaming video and digital-imaging capabilities of the units hold the potential for misuse by online child abusers and voyeurs as surveillance/anti-surveillance devices by criminals. There is also the potential for use in extortion and blackmail. There have already been reports of use in election fraud, i.e. transmitting a live picture from within the election booth.

Units may fall prey to Trojan-style attacks in an attempt to capture sensitive data either stored on the phone or transmitted via the unit, e.g. bank or card details. Such attacks have already been observed in the mobile and PDA markets over the past two years.

The increased e-mail and video-conferencing capabilities open up the possibility that criminals will use such units as secure communication tools. This is likely to rise if instant messaging services become available on 3G phones.

If such units are used to carry out voting in public elections, there is a danger that cloned or misappropriated phones could be used to skew results. This has already been a concern in Italy and Taiwan, and many countries are considering mobile-telephone-based voting systems.

There is a possibility that re-dialler programs loaded onto the phone during web surfing could redirect web access or dial premium rate lines without the user's knowledge, resulting in large telephone bills. The UK computer trade press has reported a rise in malicious re-dialler programs being disseminated, primarily by offshore premium line service pornography providers.

The use of 3G phones to access the Internet and other web services may in itself encourage a new wave of virus writing and dissemination activity, increasing resource demands on both anti-virus providers and law enforcement.

Suggested Responses

Work should begin on methodologies around the collection of evidence for use in subsequent prosecutions. This should include investigating the possibility of tracking the user's location. Further research should be targeted at capturing digital picture/video evidence, which could be based on methods used in Japan.

Law enforcement should consult and work closely with industry so that the current knowledge and expertise base can be established and maintained. This will also allow a full range of threat assessment.

Law enforcement should work with unit and service providers to explore methods for effectively blocking illegal content and services such as online child sexual abuse.

Law enforcement should work closely with unit manufacturers and service providers on anti-theft protection for units and anti-fraud systems for service providers. Means for disabling stolen units, either on the unit itself or at the service provider level, should be explored.

Law enforcement should establish liaison networks to facilitate cross-border investigations in which 3G systems are used by criminals.

Law enforcement should seek to identify a relevant working body to monitor and report on developments in connection with 3G capabilities and services. A further area of monitoring should be uptake and usage by both the general public and organized crime groups. The working body should report on developments regularly to interested parties.

MULTIMEDIA MESSAGING

Description

Multimedia messaging service (MMS) via mobile phones is a recent development which is slowly replacing short message service (SMS). The system aims at not only the exchange of messages between mobile phones but also between mobile phones and e-mail (and vice versa).

The content is not limited to text; it also comprises sound, images and other rich content. In other words, MMS enriches communication with 'real and live content'. Images or audio or video files are not attachments but appear within the body of the message as multimedia content.

In the case of pictures, sound and video such as JPEG, GIF or MP3, these files will most probably be compatible with any PC equipped with commonly available software, including Microsoft Office. Unless the files are too large, transmission is simple and does not dramatically burden the network, as it is transmitted the same way as an SMS. This system may even be able to handle short PowerPoint presentations.

Estimates from Nokia suggest that there will be enormous growth of SMS traffic in the coming years due to the advent of MMS, although at the moment compatible mobile phones are not numerous enough or widely used enough to have a significant impact.

For mobile phones without MMS capabilities, phone companies might provide users with an additional service which delivers an SMS to the recipient indicating where the MMS is stored and where it can be accessed on an Internet site. Additionally, for users without mobile phones with digital cameras or audio software installed, many optional accessories at affordable prices which can be plugged into the phone are available.

Finally, another technical solution may be installing e-mail gateway software in the phone in order to send an MMS directly to a recipient by e-mail.

Criminal Possibilities

The criminal risks related to the use of MMS are quite clear. The possibility of exchanging files in diverse forms represents a real threat to society if the content is illegal. It is easy to see how child sexual abuse images could be transmitted this way. The criminal use of this system could be very wide, e.g. the spread of viruses.

The main problem for law enforcement is the ease with which criminals could use the technology to upload, download and disseminate files with illegal content.

Another risk is anonymity: criminals can use virtually untraceable pre-paid cards for moving files and then discard them immediately after use.

Finally, the use of smart phones (as explained above) equipped with cameras may be an additional tool for criminals to disseminate illegal material.

VIRTUAL MONEY

Description

Virtual money is defined as money value as represented by a claim on the issuer which is stored on an electronic device and accepted as a means of payment by persons other than the issuer.

Virtual money is an encrypted code representing money, in the same way that paper money is only paper bearing certain characteristics such as graphics and serial numbers. Virtual money is money in the real sense since it can be converted into other forms of money. Although historically it was a slow process, people have come to accept paper money as payment, and virtual money may become dominant as electronic transactions become more common.

Like conventional paper money, virtual money can function as a medium of exchange, a unit of account and a store of value. It is intended for use in place of coins and banknotes for the purpose of making electronic payments of small amounts.

Like notes and coins, electronic cash represents ready money; it is not a credit instrument and there is no need for authorisation from a bank or credit institution. Virtual money can be carried on a number of electronic devices and may be downloaded from an automatic cash machine, a shop-based terminal or the Internet.

It can be used in the physical world by inserting a card into a terminal or through the use of wireless technology, and in the virtual world over the Internet from a PC or mobile phone or over telephone and television networks.

Many transactions over the Internet already take place with debit and credit cards. However, one of the advantages and purposes of virtual money is that it allows those individuals normally excluded from e-commerce, by reason of their economic status, for example, to participate. The cash-like nature of virtual money means that a good credit history or established banking relationship is not required. Another advantage of virtual money will be that small and new merchants can receive payment conveniently without the associated credit risks.

There are two kinds of virtual money:

- Identified virtual money - contains information

revealing the identity of the person who originally withdrew the money from the bank. This can be traced through the economy, by the bank or law enforcement personnel, in much the same way as credit cards.

- Anonymous virtual money (also known as digital cash)-once it is withdrawn from an account, it can be spent or given away without leaving a transaction trail. Using blind signatures rather than non-blind signatures creates anonymous e-money.

It is essential that the transmission of virtual money be securely encrypted, so that it cannot be read in the course of transmission.

Criminal Possibilities

The main areas of criminal risk for virtual money are believed to be:

- Unauthorised creation, transfer or redemption of virtual money.
- Criminal access to computer systems being used to change illicitly the attribution of funds within the system.
- Criminal attacks on virtual money systems, leading to loss of virtual money value or loss of function of the virtual money system.
- Criminal misuse of virtual money systems for financial crimes or as a tool to subvert or misuse other financial systems.
- Criminals may use virtual money to reduce the likelihood of capture, for example, in cases of blackmail, kidnapping or extortion, where, in the past, the collection of money has been problematic for perpetrators. This is particularly significant for anonymous virtual money.

Online games now have their own foreign exchange which lets players buy and sell different virtual currencies, just as in the real world. Criminals will undoubtedly take advantage of this.

While it is accepted within the industry that non-face-to-face transactions may give rise to new risks of money laundering, at present there is no evidence that this is a bigger concern for Internet-based companies, particularly with respect to the regulated e-money sector.

Consequences and Response

From the perspective of law enforcement, it is important to know the location of servers which provide virtual money services, especially since they may be located in a different country.

Law enforcement needs to influence legislators when drafting future legislation. This is important as law enforcement will need powers to recover data which is stored in a different jurisdiction from where the offence is being investigated.

Barriers need to be broken down and trust built up between industry and law enforcement to make service providers more accountable for data crossing their networks.

Law enforcement has to learn as a matter of urgency how to investigate crimes in which virtual money is passed to the criminal instead of real money, such as a ransom demand.

3

IT Security and Crime Prevention Methods

INTRODUCTION: GOALS AND OBJECTIVES

This document gives an introduction to what an investigator needs to know about Information Technology (IT) security measures in order to be able to carry out investigations in an IT environment and to give advice in crime prevention methods.

Information Technology plays an important and vital role in all sectors of society. As a consequence, security has become an essential component of IT.

However, it is a complex subject and the appropriate measures will often depend, to a large extent, on the type and location of the IT equipment.

The potential security threats and risks have to be carefully assessed in every situation. It is absolutely vital that all concerned are made aware of the threats and risks that may affect them, and over which they have control. Only then will they fully understand and apply the appropriate security procedures.

This report attempts to explain the various threats and risks posed by criminal activity in IT environments and offers advice about security procedures and computer crime prevention methods. It is not intended to be a comprehensive study. Threats to information systems may arise from intentional or unintentional acts and may come from internal or external sources.

This guide will address only threats, made with criminal intent, to confidentiality and integrity. Availability security functions will only be addressed if they have an effect on confidentiality and/or integrity. Examples of prevention methods will be given.

The prevention methods in this report can be used to prevent crime in companies, but can also be used to protect private computer systems.

IT Security: Definitions

CONFIDENTIALITY (Secrecy): Information and other resources are only disclosed for those 'users' (persons, entities or processes) who are authorised to have access to it.

INTEGRITY: Information and other resources are modified only by those 'users' who have the right to do so. The accuracy and completeness of the data and information is also guaranteed.

AVAILABILITY: Authorised 'users' can access information and other resources when needed.

THREAT: A 'threat' is a potential undesirable incident.

RISK: A 'risk' is the estimated probability that a 'threat' will be activated.

Information Processing and IT Security

In order to protect the data held on a computer system, various steps have to be taken: individual users should only be able to read the information which is needed to do their job; they should only be able to modify information which is specifically their job to modify. Finally, some information should not be accessible at all for individual users, e.g. the various log records.

In simple terms, information processing involves the following types of operation:

- READ/CREATE/MODIFY/DELETE information
- TRANSPORT (in one way or another) of information
- STORE information (on computer 'media' to keep it somewhere).

i. READ/CREATE/MODIFY/DELETE

Information is 'Read/Created/Modified/Deleted' by a 'User'. A 'User' is a person or a process (e.g. a computer program). Authorisation to 'Read' information is a question of confidentiality while 'Create/Modify/Delete' is primarily a question of integrity.

ii. TRANSPORT

One of the simplest ways of 'transporting' information is the internal transport between the keyboard, the memory and the hard disk in a Personal Computer. Another is the external 'transport' of a diskette from one place to another. Information can also be 'transported' using a 'Local Area Network' (LAN) and/or a 'Wide Area Network' (WAN). Insecure 'transport' affects both confidentiality and integrity.

A special kind of undesirable 'transport' is 'Electronic Emission' (see below).

iii. STORE Information

Once the information has been 'stored' on some kind of media (diskettes, tapes etc.), it may become the target of unauthorized activities which will have an effect on the confidentiality and/or integrity of the information.

Important IT Security Functions

As well as knowledge of computer architecture, the investigator also needs to be familiar with a number of important IT security functions and organizational matters if she/he is to be able to give advice on prevention methods and conduct investigations.

Some important functions are:

- Information classification
- Documentation rules
- Administration and personnel
- User Identification and Authorisation
- Logging
- Back-up
- Firewalls
- Intrusion Detection System (IDS)
- Incident Handling (IH)

Information Classification

It is essential to classify the information according to the appropriate level of availability, e.g. 'open', 'confidential', 'secret' or 'top secret'. Only then will it be possible to apply the most effective security measures. The classification should be carried out by the management or by the 'information owner'.

Documentation

All systems, but especially the 'Identification and Authorisation system', 'Information Classification system' and 'Application systems', must be fully documented.

IT security policy and the security rules for the organisation as well as details of contingency plans in the event of a major incident should be documented in a 'Security Handbook'. The chapter on IT security should have separate sections for each user category, e.g. 'Management', 'System Administrators', 'End Users' etc.

Create a checklist with guidelines concerning the actions which have to be taken in case of an incident (e.g. immediate reaction, who to contact). See chapter 'Incident Handling'.

Administration and Personnel

Success in information security work depends first and foremost on developing good basic working practices and establishing procedures to ensure that they are maintained. It is also important to create a security-conscious atmosphere and establish a disciplined approach.

If confidential information is to be handled, it is essential that the people chosen for the job are absolutely reliable. They should be security screened to a level equal to the highest level of confidential information they are likely to be asked to work on.

Access to information should be restricted to that which the individual 'needs to know' to do his job. Particularly sensitive material should be split into sections that only authorised staff can handle; no member of staff should have access to all the information.

Furthermore, security measures will only be effective if staff are properly trained. It is essential that they understand the problem. This can be achieved with in-house training.

The individual users must be trained how to use the network, how to handle confidential information, making back-ups etc. Employees can be taught what to do to counter certain threats, what they should not do, whom they can call and where they can get help. It is also very important to encourage employees to report incidents so that steps can be taken to prevent any further damage.

New or temporary employees should be given introductory training, during which data security and data integrity can be explained. It might also be useful to consider including a clause on security and confidentiality obligations in employees' contracts.

(a) Management Responsibilities

To achieve functional and cost-effective IT security, a number of initial steps must be taken by the management:

Risk Analysis : What are the threats and what is the risk that they will be activated? Threats and risks, acceptable or unacceptable, vary between different organizations. It is important to analyse the risks to make it possible for the management to form a policy with their security intentions.

Policy : There must be an Information security policy written and approved by management. No management approved policy means no resources. It should include the main security targets, information classification principles, responsible persons, and principles to reach the targets.

Security Plan : A plan has to be made to define how the targets and the intentions in the policy document should be realised. A priority list must be set up because it may not be possible to realise everything in the policy at the same time. The plan is a living document and has to be scrutinised by the IT security officer.

Security Architecture : With the risk analysis, the policy and the plan as a base, security architecture must be chosen. Security architecture is a high level description of technical security functions and organisational needs to fulfil the security demands.

Implementation : With the security architecture as a base, different security functions and products must be selected to implement the security architecture.

The main points requiring attention are:

i. All senior management, and not just the computer security manager, should be sufficiently familiar with the computer systems in use, to enable them to know what is going on and why.

ii. The role of the system manager is crucial. He/she must be of the highest degree of integrity, and sufficiently computer literate to be able to administer the system in a secure and responsible manner. The system manager access level should be restricted to the minimum number of staff required. However it must be possible for the IT security manager to check on the system manager's activities.

iii. The only way of establishing how a problem has occurred, whether the origin is accidental or deliberate, is to examine the logging information stored on the computer. (One of the reasons for restricting privileges is that the logging information of the system is available at this level). Analysis of this information should show when, where and how the problem occurred. In some cases careful examination will also indicate who was responsible. It is essential therefore that the logging capabilities of the particular system are fully understood and utilised. If the logging functions on the system are inadequate, consideration should be given to acquiring suitable software.

(b) User Responsibilities

Users should be given specific guidelines about what they should do - and more importantly - what they should not do. These guidelines should be distributed in written form, and signed for. This will counter the defence that they were unaware of the contents of the guidelines and at the same time provide the investigator with written proof.

Specimen guidelines are given below. They are certainly not exhaustive and others can be added to take account of particular circumstances.

1. Do not use any computer equipment without permission.
2. Do not try to access information unless you know you are authorised to do so.
3. Do not alter any information on a computer system unless you know you are authorised to do so. (It is also important to provide a clear written statement of what information each user is allowed to access, to whom that information may be disclosed and what action will be taken if the rules are broken.)
4. Do not use a company or authority computer for personal matters without permission.
5. Do not leave a working computer unattended, without using security options that demand retyping a password (e.g. screen saver password).
6. Make sure you know what to do in the event of a virus being discovered on the system. Use virus protection programs.
7. Be aware of malicious program code, when loading files, mails etc. from the internet or other media.
8. Keep your password and user-ID confidential.
9. Do not allow anyone else to use your password. (If people like engineers need access to the system, they should be referred to the system manager.)
10. Do not use anyone else's password.
11. Remember that anything done on the system using your ID and password can be your responsibility.

User Identification and Authorisation

Access to a computer can be restricted by means of controls based on various kinds of 'Identification and Authorisation' systems.

Identification is a two step function: (a) to Identify the user and (b) to Authenticate (validate) the identity (i.e. confirm that it is true).

The simplest systems rely on passwords only. More sophisticated systems use cards (e.g. 'SmartCard') and/or 'biometric' methods in combination with passwords.

Identification

(a) Password Systems

These give some measure of protection against casual browsing of information, but will rarely stop a determined criminal. A computer password acts like a key to a computer. Allowing several people to use the same password is like everyone using the same key.

Passwords should:

1. Be issued to an individual and kept confidential, they should not be shared with anyone. (The golden rule is ONE PERSON ONE PASSWORD). Should a temporary user need access to a system, it is usually fairly simple to add to the list of authorised users; once the temporary user has finished his work, his user-ID must be deleted from the system.)
2. Be distinct from the user-ID.
3. Ideally be:
   a. alphanumeric and
   b. at least six characters long.
4. Be changed regularly, at least every 30 days. It is

possible to warn the user automatically when his password expires. To ensure that he enters a new one, he will not be able to enter the system after the expiration date, although he may be allowed a limited number of 'grace' log-ins.

5. Be properly managed. This will involve:

   - Using a password history list, giving all the passwords used in the past year or two. New passwords will be checked against the list and not accepted if they have already been used.

     a. Making a list of frequently used passwords such as names, brands and other words that are easy to guess and therefore not suitable as passwords. This list will be used in the same way as the history list, except that new passwords will not be added; only the system manager will be able to change the list. Some systems conform to these standards and generate passwords automatically.

6. Be removed immediately if an employee leaves the organisation or gives notice of leaving.

Last but not least it is important to note that care should be taken with the password used for remote maintenance. Standard passwords which are often used to get access to different systems, for maintenance purposes, should always be avoided.

(b) Other Identification Systems

The 'password' method is built on something you 'know' and might be misused by someone getting hold of the password. A system built on something you 'know' (password, PIN-code etc.) AND something you 'have' (i.e. authorisation card) is a much stronger system. Even if someone gets hold of your password it is useless without the card. Today, the strongest method is something you 'know', something you 'have' and something you 'are' (biometrics).

There are two main types of card:

a. Magnetic strip card: As its name suggests, this type of card has a magnetic strip containing some confidential information to be used together with the holder's personal code;

b. Chip card: Instead of a magnetic strip, the card has a built in microchip. The simplest type contains a memory chip (e.g. telephone cards) containing some information but has no processing capability. The other, better, type is the 'Active' (or 'Smart') Card. It contains a microchip with both a memory to store some information and a processor. It is often used in combination with cryptographic techniques.

Biometric systems make use of specific personal characteristics (biometrics) of a specific person e.g. fingerprint, voice, keystroke characteristics or the 'pattern' of the retina. Biometric systems are still quite expensive (except for the keystroke system) and not very common.

However, even these sophisticated techniques are not infallible.

Authorisation

After identification and authentication of the user (subject) there must be a function and set of rules to control what object (files, devices etc.) each user is allowed to access. This is the Access Control system.

Logging

Most computer systems have some kind of log. Even stand-alone systems sometimes have identification and authorisation systems (and a log) if different users, with different authorisation levels, use them and/or when it is desirable to prevent users from using the disk drive (as an anti-virus measure) or changing files.

In a multi-user system (client-server-, mini-, mainframe-systems) there are always logging functions and there is often more than one kind of log.

The desired level of protection will only be achieved if the various security measures are properly followed up with a log that can be analysed as and when necessary. A proper log will answer the questions:

- WHO (user)
- WHEN (time - date)
- WHERE (place)
- WHAT (event/activity)
- ADDITIONAL (Additional information depending on activity)

There are often many different types of logs, e.g.:

- HISTORY files (e.g. Internet activities)
- TEMPORARY files
- SYSTEMS log
- TRANSACTION log
- SECURITY SYSTEM log
- DATABASE log
- APPLICATION log
- TECHNICAL log (mainly on mainframes)

Log information is one of the most important items for a computer crime investigator to look for.

Back-up

Although modern computer systems are generally very reliable, breakdowns and failures do occur, and users can make mistakes that lead to the accidental destruction of information.

To guard against total loss of information under these circumstances, it is necessary to set up procedures for making regular copies. The information on the computer system should be copied to some form of back-up medium. This medium can then be stored in a safe place until it is needed.

For particularly valuable information several copies should be made, and each copy stored in a different place and at least in different buildings, if not different cities.

The frequency with which back-ups are taken should be based on the frequency with which the information changes, the relative value of the information, and the problems its loss would cause. Regular back-up of data and system files are an essential security measure. When combined with the logging information, they should provide a comprehensive security information package. The following guidelines may be of assistance when making back-ups:

i. Make sure that regular back-up copies are made of both data and system files.

ii. Back-up cycles should be of sufficient length to be of some use in the future. 24-hour overwrite cycles are not recommended.

iii. Take a full back-up (both system and data) out of the cycle on a regular basis and archive it off site for an extended period.

iv. Back-up tapes/diskettes should be kept in a safe place under lock and key and away from the computer and where they are secured from fire, flood, magnetic and electric fields etc., preferably off site.

v. Periodically test the back-up to ensure that the information can actually be restored in an emergency; do not wait for disaster to strike to find the back-up system does not work.

Back-ups (including old ones) are another important source of information for an investigator.

Firewalls

One frequently asked question is 'how to secure the internal network from an external network such as the Internet?' One solution is to set up a firewall system.

'A firewall is a system or group of systems that enforces an access control policy between two networks. The actual means by which this is accomplished varies widely, but in principle, the firewall can be thought of as a pair of mechanisms: one, which exists to lock traffic, and the other that exists to permit traffic.

Some firewalls place a greater emphasis on blocking traffic, while others emphasise permitting traffic. Probably the most important thing to recognise about a firewall is that it implements an access control policy. If you don't have a good idea what kind of access you want to permit or deny, or you simply permit someone or some product to configure a firewall based on what they or it think it should do, then they are making policy for your organisation as a whole.' (The Internet Firewall FAQ)

Firewall systems are typically the first line of defence between an internal network (ex. of companies but also private networks) and the outside world, especially its connection to the Internet. It should be configured not only to allow certain operations to occur (FTP, mail delivery, etc), but to make it difficult or impossible for an attacker on the outside to use the firewall to penetrate the internal nets.

There are primarily two types of firewall systems, the packet-filtering firewall system and the application-level gateway.

The major difference between the two techniques lies in the flow of communication. A packet-filter gateway acts as a router between the two networks; as packets flow from their source to the destination, the gateway either forwards or blocks the packets.

With application gateways, all packets are addressed to a user-level application on the gateway that relays the packets between the two communication points.

Firewall System Requirements

Firewall systems must support features that will do the following:

- Prevent unauthorized users from accessing the internal network.
- Prevent unwanted IP service requests from being passed through it to the internal network.
- Log its activities.
- Be easy to administer.
- Provide alarm mechanisms.
- Preferably support SNMP.
- Be configurable at the user, service, and IP host level.

Security Policy

If a firewall system will be deployed to secure the access to the Internet, the configuration of the firewall system must reflect the security policy of the organization. The security policy must address, as a minimum, the following questions:

What is the policy on IP addresses?

Is the organization's IP address space a registered IP address?

Who is or will be the organisation's Internet service provider?

What is the Internet service provider's security policy? Is their network secure?

Will firewall systems be used to secure the connection to the Internet?

If so, what type of firewall system?

What is the firewall system architecture?

All entry and exit points to the Internet need to be identified. The firewall network architecture must be defined to control authorised inbound and outbound connections.

What is the policy for inbound access to systems?

Which specific protocols will be allowed to access nodes on the internal network?

What is the policy on outbound access to nodes on the Internet?

Do remote offices or branches connect to the home office?

If so, are remote offices directly connected to the Internet or is their access to the Internet through the home office?

If there is a direct connection between the remote office and the Internet, verify that if the security of the remote office is compromised, the security of the corporate network is not compromised.

Are there external networks that are not trusted?

Are there external networks that do need access to the internal network via the Internet?

Intrusion Detection Systems (IDS)

Do I need an Intrusion Detection System if I have a firewall?

Yes, the main purpose with a firewall is to protect against unauthorized external attacks but it will normally leave the network unprotected from internal attacks or intrusions. Firewalls sometimes fail to protect from external intrusions because:

- It is hard to configure the firewall properly
- Hacker/Crackers can get some packets through most firewalls and firewalls don't know what happens once someone gets through them
- The software contains a software bug (software always has bugs)
- Bad protocols can be blocked by the firewall but HTTP is allowed through and 'hack' in HTTP will pass through
- The firewall can only protect against known problems

An intruder is somebody attempting to break into or misuse the system. Intruders can be divided into two categories:

- Outsiders - Intruders from outside your own network who try to attack your system via dial-up lines, the Internet, a vendor or other 'partner' etc.
- Insiders - Intruders that are authorised to use your internal network but are misusing their privileges.

There are different types of IDS. Two main types are:

- Statistical detection - The IDS looks for deviations

from statistical measures to detect unusual behaviour. A set of variables is defined for subject and objects such as servers, files, users and other resources. A 'normal' value is set for each variable by looking at historical data or by setting expected values. When system activities occur, the list of variables is maintained and updated for each subject or object.

- Pattern (or signature) matching detection - This type of IDS compares activities against a collection of known attacks or a set of rules. The main idea is to watch for events that matches one of the patterns or violates the rules.

Why should I use a firewall and an IDS? Because most attacks come from inside and every company or organisation needs a well managed single point of entry as well. In addition, a Firewall can keep hackers running automated intrusion programs out of the internal network. Otherwise those programs can detect and exploit holes in your security architecture. There is a lot of information explaining different IDS on the Internet.

INCIDENT HANDLING SYSTEM

Even if you have installed a firewall and an Intrusion Detection System someone has to take care of an incident when it occurs (not 'if' it occurs, because it will happen sooner or later). To be well prepared is the best way to handle an incident. It is very important to stay calm and not panic when an incident occurs. It is also very important to have a special form to register incidents.

For example the SANS Institute has a step by step method for incident handling and the latest information can be obtained from the Internet at address ih@sans.org. Their method has six stages:

- preparation
- detection
- containment
- eradication
- recovery
- follow-up

Preparation: This stage covers things like policy, management support, training and interfaces to law enforcement.

Identification: How to identify an incident, responsible staff, coordination with network suppliers, etc.

Containment: Create the on-site team to survey the situation. Backup of the system. Risk determination (to let the system run) etc.

Eradication: Perform vulnerability analysis. Remove the cause of the incident, etc

Recovery: Restore the system. Validate the system, etc

Follow-up: Develop a follow-up report.

COMPUTER ARCHITECTURE

The main types of computer architecture are indicated below. In many cases, the specific threats and risks to which a particular system is exposed will depend on its architecture. However, there are a number of threats which can affect all systems, irrespective of their architecture.

Main architecture types

- Microcomputers
- Network architectures and mini computers
- Mainframes
- Hand-held computers.

Microcomputers (stand-alone)

These computers have no facilities for permanent external communications, apart from links to peripherals (e.g. printer, scanner, streamer, extra disk drive etc.). Nowadays it is common to have a modem and a temporary connection to the Internet.

This architecture is easiest to 'protect' but it is also the architecture where the users are least aware of the possible threats and risks. If it is connected to the Internet it can be vulnerable to external attacks if it is not properly configured. The user is responsible for back-ups, keeping media in a safe place, protecting data from unauthorized access, etc.

Examples:

Personal Computer (IBM PC-compatible) - Desktop, Laptop

Macintosh, Amiga, etc.

Network Architectures and Mini Computers

A mini computer is linked to several workstations to serve a limited number of users. The workstations may consist of just a keyboard and screen, or microcomputers (so-called 'intelligent' terminals) may be used.

Today, these mini computers are often referred to as 'servers' linked to their workstations through a Local Area Network (LAN). Commonly known as client-server architecture.

In many organizations the old mainframe architecture is now being replaced with a number of 'servers' each of which has a different set of functions. Connections from the LAN to Wide Area Networks (WAN) are common.

The user is only responsible for backing up the files on the hard disk on his own workstation (if it has one). One or more administrators are responsible for all other back-ups, loading new programs etc. Management of the network is normally left to a Network Administrator.

Examples:

UNIX-systems, OS/2-servers, and IBM AS400

Digital Micro VAX, etc.

Mainframes

Used in big organisations to serve a great number of users and/or where considerable computing capacity is needed. A special computer room with air conditioning is needed, too. This is often located in a restricted area of the building and specialists are required to operate the computer. Network operators monitor the communication functions and assist users if there are communication problems.

System development and programming is a task for specialised staff. The user is only responsible for backing up the files on the hard disk of his workstation (if it has a disk). Because of the very fast technical development in the field of client-server it is today not possible to clearly define the difference between mainframes and servers.

Hand-held Computers

This type of computers, like personal organizers, is completely different from the others and is discussed in section 'Technical devices & communications' in the Interpol Computer Crime Manual. The most important prevention method is to keep the equipment in a safe place and away from unauthorized persons.

THREATS AND CRIME PREVENTION METHODS

This section gives examples of the threats that may occur. Some may be encountered in all types of environment, others may only occur with specific types of computer architecture.

The prevention methods mentioned are only given as examples. The risk of the threat being activated must be assessed in each organisation and depends on factors such as the company's information policy, employees' awareness, etc.

In the following tables, the various threats to which a system may be exposed are grouped according to where the information is located in the IT process.

READ/CREATE/MODIFY/DELETE refers to information (data and software) inside the computer system.

TRANSPORT refers to information (data and software) 'transported' via a network or on media.

STORE refers to information (data and software) when it is stored on computer media and taken out of the computer system. (I.e. back-up tapes/diskettes).

Architecture-independent Threats

There are a number of important 'architecture-independent security targets':

- Members of staff, with certain responsibilities, powers, information
- Media handling
- Malicious programs
- Electronic emission

Members of Staff

Disloyal staff

See advice given above in 'Important IT security functions'.

The strongest form of security is often procedural security with attendant staff awareness and responsibility.

Unauthorized access to information by users

Users should be given specific written guidelines on what they should and should not do. Guidelines should be signed for.

Install an 'Identification and Authorisation' system. Adopt a 'two-man rule' for granting privileges.

Do not reveal your password too anyone.

Keep identification and authorisation cards in a safe place.

Regularly check logs.

Regularly check that configuration is correct.

Install an Intrusion Detection System.

See above, chapter 'Important IT security functions'

Unauthorized access to information by system administrators, programmers, etc.

The same as above and:

Use separate systems for program development and for 'production'.

Restrict access to equipment with sensitive information; adopt 'two-man rule'.

Restrict use of 'super user'/'root' privileges.

Unauthorized access to information by temporary staff, e.g. consultants, service engineers etc.

As for other staff and:

Limit their access to the system to the time and day required for the specific task.

Do not forget to cancel their access rights and close their temporary accounts.

Do not leave communication lines for remote servicing open when not needed.

Unauthorized Access from External Sources

Unauthorized access.

Install an 'Identification and Authorisation' system. Adopt a 'two-man rule' for granting privileges.

Regularly check logs.

Regularly check that configuration is correct. Install a firewall.

See above chapter 'Important IT security functions'

Media Handling

Total loss of information through theft of media

Media should be kept in a safe place under lock and key.

Loss (by copying or transfer) of information as a result of unauthorized access to, or loan of, media

Encrypt sensitive information. Staff handling the media should not have access to the encryption keys.

'Two-man rule' for back-up.

'Two-man rule' for access to archives.

Loss (by copying or transfer) of information during servicing

Never send equipment with sensitive information on mounted media for servicing.

(It is not enough to 'Delete' sensitive information because of 'Undelete /unerase' possibilities)

Malicious Program Code

Viruses and other malicious programs.

Install 'anti-virus software'. See Chapter 'Investigations', Section 'Malicious program code' in the Interpol Computer Crime Manual.

Programs altered to obtain access to, or manipulate, information without authorisation.

Depends on computer architecture.

Use separate systems for program development and for 'production'.

If possible, restrict access to 'source code', 'compilers' and 'editors' in 'production' system and restrict use or installation of non-standard software packages.

An Intrusion Detection System might detect this type of problem. See above chapter 'Important IT Security functions'

Electronic Emission

Despite all precautions, it is still possible for a determined intruder to eavesdrop on information by picking up and interpreting electromagnetic emissions from the Personal Computer or workstation.

In a manner somewhat similar to the way in which it is possible to detect the operation of a television receiver and determine which channel is being watched. This type of eavesdropping is most likely to occur when very sensitive information, such as that of high commercial value or dealing with matters of national security is involved.

Use equipment with no or limited signal leakage ('tempest') or put the equipment in a shielded room. Although effective, those methods are expensive and are only to be recommended when there is an extremely high risk. Optical fibres can be used to prevent emission leakage from the lines running between peripherals and the Local Area Network (LAN).

Encryption of the Wide Area Network (WAN) will not stop electromagnetic emissions but the eavesdropper will not be able to use the information without the encryption key.

Microcomputer (stand-alone, Personal Computer) Systems

Much sensitive information is stored on personal computer systems. The main risk is unauthorized access to that data, or that the data may become corrupted or lost.

READ/CREATE/MODIFY/DELETE

Corruption of files (program or data). A major cause of data loss and corruption is the introduction of viruses to computer systems.

Keep program diskettes write-protected at all times.

Do not keep data and software on the same diskette. Otherwise, if software becomes corrupted or infected, the data will usually be lost as well. Making files read-only will prevent them from being infected by some viruses, but not all of them. All media should be scanned for viruses before use, preferably on a system specially designated for the purpose.

Unauthorized access of information stored in the computer

Restrict physical access to the Personal Computer, by locking the door (and the machine if possible) whenever it has to be left unattended. Machines should never be left switched on and running, unless a reliable software protection mechanism has been installed.

Unauthorized use of the computer

As above.

Malicious programs (i.e. viruses)

See Chapter 'Investigations', Section 'Malicious program code' in the Interpol Computer Crime Manual.

Loss (by copying or transfer) of information during servicing

Never send equipment with sensitive information on mounted media for servicing.

(It is not enough to 'delete' sensitive information because of 'undelete/unerase' possibilities).

Theft of the computer

Restrict physical access to the Personal Computer, by locking the door (and the machine if possible) whenever it has to be left unattended.

Laptops are particularly at risk when left unattended in hotel rooms etc.

Use cryptography to protect information from unauthorized access.

TRANSPORT

Loss of confidential or secret information during transport

Transport media in sealed envelopes and/or locked boxes.

Manipulation of media during transport

As above and electronic seal (cryptologic checksum) on information.

Total loss of media during transport

Never leave media unattended in cars, hotel rooms etc.

STORE

Loss (by copying or transfer) of information

Diskettes and other media should be kept locked up in a safe place when not in use.

Physical loss of information

As above and it is advisable to install removable hard disks, which should be kept in a safe place.

Total loss of information through theft of computer and/or media

Regular back-ups of data and system files are essential. Together with the logging information, they will provide a comprehensive security information package.

Loss (by copying or transfer) of information as a result of unauthorized access to, or loan of, media

Network Architectures and Mini Computer Systems

Local Area Network (LAN)

If a Personal Computer (PC) is connected to a network, there are two other possibilities for interfering with data, in addition to the dangers of physical access to the machine (as mentioned above).

Firstly, it becomes possible to access the information stored on the PC via the network. Care should therefore be taken to ensure networking software is correctly configured, and that only that information which is intended to be generally accessible is stored in directories which can be accessed via a network.

Secondly, the danger of leaving a PC unattended is much greater: not only can the data on the PC itself be compromised, but there is also a risk that any data which the rightful user may be able to access over the network will also be compromised.

In a network environment, especially where sensitive material is in use, it is essential to keep a central record of activity, i.e. a log. This should be held on a machine that is known to be secure, and should contain a record of ALL activity on the network; there should also be a procedure for examining the log, so that all suspicious events can be highlighted and investigated.

Wide Area Network (WAN)

Networks are connected either by cable, by microwave or satellite. The latter are vulnerable to interception as are any radio transmissions unless the data is encrypted. The transmission of electronic signals is governed by standards that are called 'protocols'.

There are many standards, the most common is the TCP/IP which is the standard packet-switching protocol used for the Internet. Such connection can be protected against improper use or interception in various ways. The best way is to use Identification, Authentication and Cryptography as well as firewall and Intrusion Detection Systems (IDS).

Costs have also to be considered. Telecommunication companies can offer the use of dedicated lines - as often used by financial institutions, which means that these lines are not available for normal public use and are protected against intrusion, but they cost substantially more. This also applies to encryption.

There are a number of encryption standards and devices ranging from small logical keys installed on sending and receiving equipment to higher levels of coding which use complicated mathematical cycles and algorithms. The decision to implement such higher level systems will have to be taken in the light of the value of transmitted data.

It must also be remembered that encryption is not an infallible solution and that its use raises various problems, e.g. several countries are developing, or discussing the development of a specific law to regulate the use of encryption.

Even when communications are well protected, problems of unauthorized access can occur if a well-protected system is linked directly to another that is not protected. Any given system is only as secure as those to which it is connected.

The Internet

Victims of Internet attacks are often organizations that did not bother too much about their security or who trusted some sales person who said that the Internet connection was absolutely safe.

A lot of safeguards are mentioned above and they are applicable for the Internet as well. Some additions are:

- Do not connect computers or entire networks, which contain your critical information (e.g. financial, confidential, privacy) to the Internet.
- If possible restrict the way to the Internet to just one single point of connection.
- Do not store your password or identification number on your hard disk, protect it otherwise from unauthorized access. Create a password policy (see chapter , identification - password systems).
- Check and update your list of user accounts.
- Install a firewall system and an IDS.
- Do not download files or open emails which you do not trust.
- Install an anti-virus software and update it frequently.
- Be aware of shared-files which might be accessed of unauthorized persons.

- Be aware of cookies, Java and ActiveX applets, etc.
- Install only minimal options.

THREATS

READ/CREATE/MODIFY/DELETE

Manipulations or unauthorized access to software or information in each workstation (PC) in the network

See Microcomputer systems

Unauthorized access to information in the 'server' by users

Users should be given specific written guidelines on what they are allowed and not allowed to do. Guidelines should be signed for.

Install an 'Identification and Authorisation' system. Adopt a 'two-man rule' for granting privileges.

Regularly check logs.

Regularly check that configuration is correct. IDS should be installed.

Unauthorized access to information by system administrators, programmers' etc.

As above and:

Use separate systems for program development and for 'production'.

Restrict access to server; adopt 'two-man rule'.

Restrict use of 'super user'/'root' privileges.

Corruption of files (program or data). A major cause of data loss and corruption is the introduction of viruses to computer systems.

All media should be scanned for viruses, preferably on a system specially designated for the purpose, before use.

Erase all unnecessary codes, default and unused procedures.

Total loss of information through 'disk crash' or deliberate destruction of files

Regular back-ups of data and system files are essential. Together with the logging information, they will provide a comprehensive security information package. For back-up guidelines, see 3.6

Loss (by copying or transfer) of information during servicing

Some mini-server servicing can be done 'on-site' but in the case of some hardware problems the equipment will have to be taken away for repair by the service company/ vendor.

Never send equipment with sensitive information on media for servicing without a verifiable guarantee that the information will be destroyed. (It is not enough to 'delete' the sensitive information because of 'undelete' and 'unformat' possibilities).

Remember that after repair, the disk drives could be reused somewhere else and your information might be compromised.

If it is decided to replace a disk with sensitive information, destroy it yourself.

Theft of the server

The server should be kept locked up in a safe place.

TRANSPORT in Local Area Network (LAN)

Interception of cables

Segmentation of the LAN.

Use optical fibres.

Regularly inspect LAN.

Encrypt LAN.

Interception of networks components (like 'routers', 'bridges', 'gateways', 'repeaters' etc.)

Restrict physical access to components.

Regularly check that the configuration of each individual component is correct.

Manipulation of network components

As above.

Unapproved workstations

The system should be set up in a way that the management must approve the workstations before they can be used.

Regularly check that the configuration is correct.

Network administrator accessing user files

Network Administrators should be given specific written guidelines on what they should and should not do. Guidelines should be signed for.

Restrict use of 'administrator' privileges.

Install an 'Identification and Authorisation' system.

Adopt a 'two-man rule' for granting privileges.

Access to the LAN from 'outside'

Provide guidelines for the use of modems or other connections.

IDS and firewall should be used.

Regularly check that the configuration is correct.

TRANSPORT in Wide Area Network (WAN)

Interception of cables

Communications can be encrypted, but there may be legal restrictions.

Interception of radio communications

As above.

Intruders ('hacking'/'cracking')

Use special modems at each end, which recognise each other's signals (mutual signal recognition).

Install an 'Identification and Authorisation' system. Adopt a 'two-man rule' for granting privileges.

IDS and firewall should be used.

For password rules, User Identification and Authorisation.

TRANSPORT of Media

Loss of confidential or secret information during transport

Transport media in sealed envelopes or locked boxes. Cryptography should be used.

Manipulation of media during transport

As above and:

Electronic seal (cryptologic checksum) on information.

Total loss of media during transport

Never leave media unattended in cars etc.

STORE

Loss (by copying or transfer) of information

Media should be kept in a safe place under lock and key.

'Two-man' rule for access to archives.

Total loss of information through theft of media

Regular back-ups of data and system files are essential.

Together with the logging information, they will provide a comprehensive security information package.

Mainframe Computer Systems

There is normally some kind of access system to a mainframe via terminals or a number of LANs with workstations, which will be subject to the threats mentioned above.

In that connection, (Architecture-independent threats), (Microcomputer systems), and (Network architectures and mini computer systems), as appropriate.

THREATS

READ/CREATE/MODIFY/DELETE

Manipulations or unauthorized access to software

Use separate computers for system/program development and 'production'.

If possible, restrict access to 'source code', 'compilers' and 'editors' in 'production' system.

Unauthorized access to information

Users should be given specific written guidelines on what they should and should not do. Guidelines should be signed for.

Install an 'Identification and Authorisation' system. Adopt a 'two-man rule' for granting privileges.

IDS and firewall should be used.

Regularly check logs.

Regularly check that configuration is correct.

Unauthorized access to information by system administrators, programmers, etc.

As above and:

Separate test/development systems from production systems.

Restrict access to the computer room. 'Closed shop' for all other than those working in the computer room.

Restrict use of 'super user'/'root' privileges.

Cryptography should be used for confidential information.

Corruption of files (program or data) by malicious programs

Use 'checksums' on sensitive software to make it possible to control that it has not been changed deliberately.

Erase all unnecessary codes, default and unused procedures.

Loss (by copying or transfer) of information during servicing

Servicing of mainframe systems is done 'on site'. In the case of hardware problems with disk drives they should be replaced and the faulty ones sent to the vendor for repair, if possible.

They can later be used as replacements, perhaps at another site.

Never send equipment with sensitive information on media for servicing without a verifiable guarantee that the information will be destroyed. (It is not enough to 'delete' sensitive information because of 'undelete' and 'unformat' possibilities).

Cryptography should be used for confidential information.

TRANSPORT in Local Area Network (LAN)

(Network Architectures and Mini-computer systems)

(Network architectures and Mini-computer systems)

TRANSPORT in Wide Area Network (WAN)

(Network Architectures and Mini-computer systems)

(Network architectures and Mini-computer systems)

TRANSPORT of Media

Loss of confidential or secret information during transport

Transport media in sealed envelopes or locked boxes. Cryptography should be used for confidential information.

Manipulation of media during transport

As above and electronic seal (cryptologic checksum) on information.

Total loss of media during transport

Never leave media unattended in cars etc.

STORE

Loss (by copying or transfer) of information

Media should be kept in a safe place under lock and key.

'Two-man rule' for access to archives.

Total loss of information through theft of media

Regular back-ups of data and system files are essential. Together with the logging information, they will provide a comprehensive security information package.

4

INTERNATIONAL WORK GROUPS

The European Commission has recognised the need for a comprehensive approach to information system security to protect the individual, the business community and public administrations against increasingly sophisticated threats and combinations of threats.

Consequently, the Commission took the initiative of proposing an overall 'framework' in which information security problems could be assessed and an appropriate set of solutions identified and developed.

The evaluation of the security of information systems has been a key activity with regard to the implementation of a number of the action lines.

The European criteria ITSEC (IT Security Evaluation Criteria), and associated methodology (ITSEM), has been the subject of many of the INFOSEC projects.

The art of US evaluation criteria (TCSEC, Trusted Computer System Evaluation Criteria) is commonly known as the 'Orange Book'.

A new standard - the CC (Common Criteria) - has been adopted as new international standard and will replace ITSEC and TCSEC in a period. However, ITSEC and TCSEC will be used parallel with CC for some time.

COMPANY CHECKLIST

This Information Technology (IT) crime prevention checklist focuses on a range of IT security topics to be considered in the field of threats, with criminal intent, to Information Technology.

The checklist is just a reminder of what to consider and not an instruction on how to introduce certain security measures. Some of the topics may need assistance from experts in that field to be understood and implemented.

If this checklist is copied and distributed outside law enforcement, please fill in the name of the contact person within the police.

Police contact person:

1. Management responsibilities
2. Organization
3. Personnel (employees)
4. Personnel (other)
5. Information classification
6. Software
7. Hardware
8. Documentation
9. Computer media
10. Identification and authorization
11. System security
12. Communication
13. Logging
14. Back-up

15. Physical protection
16. Incident handling
17. Contingency planning

MANAGEMENT RESPONSIBILITIES

1. Information security policy? Does it exist and has it been written and approved by management?

   No policy = No resources.

2. Is there a process for scrutinising the policy?

   It is a living document and must be updated

3. Is there an initiative from management to do a risk analysis?

   What are the threats and the risk that they will be activated?

4. Is there a management initiative to create a security plan?

   To define how the targets and the intention in the policy document should be realised

5. Is there a management initiative to create a security architecture?

   The security architecture is a high level description of technical security functions and organizational needs to fulfil the security demands.

6. Is there any management policy for external communication like the Internet?

   Internet connections tend to grow uncontrolled

7. Do all management staff know the contents and intentions of the policy?

8. Is the organization for Information Security work defined in the policy document?
9. Is there any Information Security training plan?
10. Are Information Security topics a part of the introduction plan for new members of the staff?

ORGANIZATION

1. Is there an Information Security officer?

   Someone must have the responsibility to put the management policy into practice.

2. Does an Information Security handbook exist? has it been approved by the management?
3. Is there an organization and plan to train the staff regularly in security matters?

   Information Security training is not a once-and-for-all training.

4. Is there an organization for the 'Identification and Authorization' system?
5. Is there an organization for contingency planning and handling?
6. Is there an organization plan for handling incidents?

   The organization must be prepared for incidents

7. Is the responsibility and authority defined in the organization plan, or in a job description document?
8. Does an organization plan exist to explain the different staff categories in the IT process? E.g. IT Security Manager, Developers, Operators, Users etc.

   Different categories need different

   training and handbooks in Information

   Security matters

PERSONNEL (EMPLOYEES)

1. Are new members checked before employment? References, education, security clearance etc. Must be done before. After it might be too late.

2. Are new staff informed of secrecy regulations?

3. Do they sign a secrecy certificate?

4. Are 'key-persons'. identified?

   Backup available for those?

5. Does the staff get appropriate security training on a regular basis?

   Information Security training is not a once-and-for-all training.

6. Are all staff informed on the consequences of breaking the security regulations?

   Security violation.

7. Are there any routines for employees who leave?

   There are many things to clean up in IT- systems to remove their authorities.

   Systems Administration Personnel

8. Are they informed on specific security regulations for Developers, Network Administrators etc.?

   A 'root'-privilege does not imply they have authority to access of all data/information.

   Users

9. Are there very short, written security instructions for users?

   Maximum 1 page

PERSONNEL (OTHER)

1. Are there written contracts/agreements with Third Party companies?
2. Are those personnel categories informed about security routines?

   They should sign a document to acknowledge that they understand the rules.
3. Are those personnel categories 'security checked'?

   Security clearance
4. Are the companies they work for (their employer) 'security checked'?

   Security clearance
5. Are 'key-persons' identified?

   Backup available for those?
6. Are those personnel categories informed of the consequences of breaking the security regulations?
7. Are there any routines for end of assignments?

   There are many things to clean up in IT- systems to remove their authorities.

INFORMATION CLASSIFICATION

1. Is there a system for information classification according to the appropriate level of availability? (e.g. open, confidential, secret).

   To make it possible to apply the most effective security measures
2. Does the classification system require encryption for any class or type of information?

3. Is there a classification checklist to make it easy for the user to determine information class?

SOFTWARE

1. Are there any instructions for bringing outside software/data into the organization?
2. Are policy documents and security guidelines considered during developing systems?

   Security features must be implemented from the beginning.
3. Are security requirements included in the demand specification when buying or developing systems?

   The requirements must be included from the beginning.
4. Are system tests and development separated from production systems?

   Avoid compilers and editors in production systems.
5. Are security-related patches from developers and/or vendors implemented as soon as possible?

   Routines for this must exist.
6. Is a security validation approval done before introducing new software? Individual users should not be allowed to introduce new software.

   New software might create new holes in the system.
7. Is there a routine for installing a new operating system?

   This is the most critical software and all configuration parameters must be checked before rebooting.
8. Is it a classified operating system?

   According to ITSEC, TCSEC, Common Criteria

9. Are security options in the operating system activated?

10. Are there any routines to change all security related default parameters in the operating system?

11. Is it the same type of routine for application software?

    To change defaults and to set security parameters.

12. Are additional (e.g. hacks) and self-developed software well documented?

13. Are there any routines to request all patches that are needed to preserve the security?

    To prevent hacking possibilities.

14. Are 'system-tools' protected?

    Software to administer and service the system.

15. Are the use of 'system-tools' restricted to just a few persons?

16. Is all use of 'system-tools' logged?

17. Is anti-virus software installed and activated?

18. Do the users know how to handle viruses?

19. Are there any extended controls of software downloaded from WAN such as Internet?

20. Are the users informed about software licenses, as to what extent they are allowed to copy them and use them in other equipment? If they are allowed to use them for private use at home etc.?

21. Is loading of new software regulated?

22. Is critical software backed up and stored in another safe place?

23. Is critical software protected by checksums.

24. Is all software from well-known sources?

    Special notice on encryption software

HARDWARE

1. Are there any instructions for bringing equipment outside the organization?
2. Are there instructions on how to discard equipment?
3. Is it made clear that the equipment is for business use only and not for private use by the user?

4 Are policy documents and security guidelines considered during introduction of new equipment?

5 Are security requirements included in the demand specification when buying or changing equipment?

The requirements must be included from the beginning.

6 Is a security validation made before introducing new hardware?

New hardware might create new holes in the system.

7 Is there a person responsible for each workstation/ personal computer?

DOCUMENTATION

1 Is the management policy document printed and distributed to all members of staff and subsequently to new members?

2 Is there an Information Security handbook?

3 Are systems and manual routines well documented?

To prevent the dependence on key- persons.

4 Are there documents describing:

- Hardware
- Software
- Applications
- Communication

Are they up to date?

5 Do handbooks for each staff category exist?

- Developer
- Administrators (network, database etc.)
- Users
- Helpdesk etc.

6 Are there any written rules defining responsibility and authority for each staff category?

7 Are system documents stored in a safe place?

8 Is the access to the system documents restricted?

Computer Media

1 Are there any routines for labelling media?

2 Are all media listed in an inventory?

3 Are media handed over with receipts?

4 Is the existence of media checked on a regular base? Media in the inventory list.

5 Are there any routines to handle missing media?

6 Are there any routines for archiving media?

7 Are there any routines for transporting media?

8 Are there any routines for destroying media?

9 Are there any routines for how to handle media during service?

Don't leave media unattended during service and don't let media with secret information leave your organization

Identification and Authorisation

1 Is there an Identification/Authorisation system that controls both users and resources?

Should be.

2 Is the system built on 'something you know and something you have'?

A system with both password/PIN and something the users have (Smart- card/Biometrics) is preferable.

3 Does the system include logging and alarm functions?

Preferable. Necessary to be able to trace incidents and to get quick alerts.

4 Is there an organization to administer the Identification/Authorisation system?

Shouldn't be the computer department.

5 Does the system include access control to resources/ objects?

6 Is it quality tested on password/PIN?

Don't allow too short passwords/PIN codes or codes with just alphabetic or numeric characters.

7 Is it possible to reuse old passwords/PIN?

Shouldn't be.

8 Is it possible to use the user ID as password/PIN?

Shouldn't be.

9 Are there any routines to change software default passwords?

Most software, including the operating system has a lot of defaults known by a lot of people. Must be changed.

10 Is the number of log in attempts limited?

Should be to prevent hacking.

11 Is the change of password/PIN compulsory after a certain number of days?

Should be.

12 Is the system administrator password (root) changed frequently?

Should be.

13 Does the system block an account if the password is not changed within the time limit or the account has been remained unused?

Should be.

14 Is it possible for a user to change their own privileges?

Shouldn't be.

15 Is the password/PIN encrypted? (one way encryption)

Should never be transported or stored in an unencrypted way.

16 Is the user authentication so called 'strong' authentication?

Preferable.

17 Is the password/PIN individual?

Must be.

SYSTEM SECURITY

1 Is there a routine to ensure the correct date and time in all systems and are they synchronised?

2 Are there enhanced logging facilities in critical systems?

COMMUNICATION

1 Are there documented procedures for changing the network?

2 Are all changes to the network documented?

3 Is access to communication ports for service protected?

4 Is the network administrator privilege restricted to a few users?

5 Is all network hardware (HUB, Repeaters, Routers, Gateways etc.) well protected?

6 Is the software in the network hardware well protected? Use strong authentication for changing the software or configuration.

7 Is an IDS (Intrusion Detection System) installed?

To prevent 'insiders' from doing unauthorised things. Will not replace the need for a firewall.

External

8 Is a firewall installed?

9 Is there a routine for the administration of the firewall?

Setting up a firewall is not a once-and-for-all job. It must be updated constantly.

10 Is the use of encryption considered?

Is there a trustworthy algorithm and key administration?

11 Is access to communication ports for service protected?

Are the safeguards (including encryption when needed) considered regarding:

12 - E-mail

13 - Telnet

Strong authentication

14 - FTP

15 - PPP

16 - EDI

17 - SNMP

18 - DNS-services

19 - Routing

20 - Web-sessions

21 - Java, Javascript

22 - ActiveX

23 - Finger

24 - Rlogin

25 - Cookies

26 Are closed user group used?

27 Are VPN (Virtual Private Networks) used?

Logging

1 Is the logging system documented?

2 Are the log files protected against unauthorised access?

3 Is the system configured in a way that the log must be turned on?

What events are logged:

4 Login

5 Logout

6 Failed login

7 Exceptional behaviour

User not acting normaly.

Might be sorted out via an IDS

8 Access violation

Unauthorised access to resources

9 Activities in the Identification and Authorisation system?

New users, change of privileges, remove of users etc.

10 Setting of date and time

11 Introduction/removal of new hardware

12 Introduction/removal of new software

13 Introduction/removal of files

14 Are the log-files archived in a proper way?

Back-up

1 Are backups taken on a regular basis?

2 Are backups stored and archived in safe place?

According to unauthorised access and 'climate' (fire, water etc.)

3 Are the backup routines documented?

4 Are the backups labelled?

5 Is encryption of backups considered for secret information?

Physical Protection

1 Are all premises protected?

2 Are computers and network components placed in an access-protected area?

3 Is all system documentation safeguarded?

4 Are communication lines protected?

5 Is there an admission and leaving control system with a log?

6 Are the premises divided in different zones?
To restrict access

7 Is there an up to date list with authorised people?

Incident Handling

1 Is there a plan for how to handle incidents?

2 Do you know the police unit responsible for computer crime?

Contingency Planning

1 Is there a contingency plan? How to recover the system after an incident

FREQUENTLY ASKED QUESTIONS

1. What is the biggest threat to information security for companies?

One big threat occurs if your staff are unaware of the importance of information security and the difference between 'nice to know' and 'need to know'.

Employees should only have access to the information that they need in order to do their job (to prevent information leakage).

Your staff must be informed about IT security and trained regularly. A key threat for companies is hacking. Hackers not only destroy data, they can also destroy the image and the reputation of the company too.

2. What can we do, to secure our permanent Internet connection and local network against hacking, data spying, data altering etc.?

The solution is called firewall. A firewall is able to defend hacking attempts in a computer system, but it is necessary to administrate the system every time. Normally, a firewall will only protect against unauthorised access from outside. It should be complemented by an Intrusion Detection System (IDS) system. An IDS will protect the system from internal attacks and failure of the firewall.

Introduce an Incident Handling System (IHS). Being well prepared is the best condition in order to minimise the damage and losses after an incident.

To keep out unauthorised persons it is further recommended to use access codes as passwords. Passwords should not be too short or too easy to find out and they should be changed frequently.

3. What shall I do, if I recognise that a hacker is attacking my computer system now?

With an IHS you will be prepared to handle the incident. If you do not have an IHS and you recognise that a hacker has attacked a computer system, the best thing to do is disconnect the system from the net.

Further, it is usually necessary to make a seizure of the attacked system and of the log protocols. It is important to make a full back-up so that evidence (i.e. IP-address, login-time) can be collected. If there is a serious threat or damage, it is recommended that it should be reported to the police.

4. How can I secure my stand-alone PC and data against unauthorised access?

To secure a stand-alone PC it is recommended to set up a BIOS-password and a screensaver-password. It is necessary to change passwords frequently. Encryption can be used to protect important/confidential information.

There are different methods of protecting a PC physically, such as alarm systems, floppy locks, etc.

5. How can I protect a computer system from computer viruses?

A very simple and useful method against computer viruses is to use a anti-virus program (like Norton Anti-Virus or McAffee). A problem is that new viruses are created very fast and so it is necessary to update the anti-virus program frequently. It is also dangerous to download data from unknown sources and open e-mails from unknown persons. Special attention should be given to attachments to mail. Use a stand-alone PC to check diskettes for viruses before they are loaded into the network.

It is important to have a company policy that explains that uncontrolled downloading can have undesirable consequences, because of the risk of viruses.

6. How can I transmit confidential electronic information to a receiver?

If it is really necessary to transmit confidential information via e-mail, it is recommended that you should use an encryption program like Pretty Good Privacy (PGP).

7. How can I bring awareness to the employees and management in my organization?

Tell your management what can happen in the case of uncontrolled internal access to information or lack of protection from external attacks. If a hacker successfully attacks your company network, inform the management about possible material damages and the loss of reliability and image. Educate employees and management to never give their PIN numbers, password, and calling card numbers to anyone.

8. What should we do if external persons service our system?

The best way is to save the confidential information on other media before servicing. Furthermore, it is recommended to observe the persons during the servicing, if they have not been security checked before. Never let external service staff take computer media or computers with classified information from your site.

9. How can I protect a telecommunication system from misuse such as unauthorised access?

Normally a mobile phone or a fix phone can be protected against misuse with a Personal Identification Number (PIN). In a large telecommunication system (like those in companies) it is recommended to block special telephone numbers (like audiotex lines), which produces higher charges.

10. Where can I get information about IT Security?

There are a lot of publications, books, training courses etc., covering these topics. Information can also be obtained from the Internet as well as from IT security companies. Some basic information can be obtained from your local police organisation and there are many websites on the topic.

PRIVATE CHECKLIST

Advice for private use of computers

1. Theft of computers

2. Malicious program code (virus, worms, Trojan horses etc.)
3. Protect your data from unauthorised access
4. Misuse of your Internet account
5. Electronic commerce
6. Software piracy
7. Employer's information
8. "Illegal" information
9. Anonymity on the Internet
10. Backup

1. Theft of Computers

Theft of computers is very common. Companies often install safety doors, alarm systems and use data safes for backups. At home, employees' computers are much more vulnerable.

Advice: Don't expose your computer unnecessarily. If it can be seen through the window you might be the next victim if a thief explores your neighbourhood. Use removable hard disks. You can then put your disk away in a safe place if you are going to leave your computer unattended for a longer period. It is recommended that you protect your data with encryption, so that no one can read your private data.

2. Malicious program codes (virus, worms, Trojan horses etc.)

One specific type of virus program is the Trojan Horse that creates possibilities for others to take control of your system (backdoors). Programs like NetBus, Back Orifice, Bubbles, Back Door etc., make it possible for an intruder to take control of your computer.

Advice: Install "Anti-virus software" and don't forget to update it continuously. Obtain information from your ISP, software supplier, CERT (Computer Emergency Response Team)- organisations on how to detect such malicious programs. They all have information on the Internet to support you. If you are a victim - disconnect from the net and clear your computer of the malicious program. Take back-ups of your user data frequently because there are no 100 % reliable anti-virus tools.

3. Protect your data from unauthorised access

Advice : To protect your data from unauthorised access it is recommended that you use a BIOS-password and a screen-saver-password. If you have sensitive data there are methods to encrypt the whole disk online (data will always be stored on the disk in encrypted format).

A useful method to secure data from unauthorised people is to keep them away from it. If it is necessary to transmit such files via e-mail or the postal service you cannot be sure that no one, other than the authorised person, can get access to it or is able to read it. In those cases a recommended measure is to work with encryption programs.

One of the most famous cryptography program is Pretty Good Privacy, better known as PGP, but a lot of other good programs are in existence, and may be found on the Internet. Be sure that you get the programs from trustworthy sources

With these kinds of programs it is possible to secure e-mails, hard disks, folders or only a normal file like a Word-document.

4. Misuse of your Internet account

It is quite popular to attempt to get hold of other users' accounts on the Internet. The main purpose is to avoid billing or to act with other people's identity for different reasons.

Advice: Change passwords frequently and do not use to short or simple passwords. Use the principle one person one password. Don't even share your password with the rest of your family. You can't be sure what your kids and their friends are doing. This is very important if you are using Internet banking. If something goes wrong, your bank will probably not accept losses if you share your password with someone else, even if it is a family member.

5. *Electronic commerce*

Many people use the Internet for buying goods like books, CDs etc.

Advice: Preferably use only systems with specific safeguards. Never buy goods by giving your credit card number and the expiration date without encryption on the Internet (be sure that it is a trusted service - normally you can see the key image for using encryption on your screen). Always check your bills from credit card companies and banks. Be aware, when you are using your credit card in a point-of-sale system in a shop, most of the card information will be printed at the receipt. Don't leave the receipt in the shop, bring it with you.

6. *Software piracy*

Copyright laws in most countries cover computer software.

Advice: Be sure you only use software you are authorised to use. If you are not sure about software from your employer, - ask the IT person responsible at your place of work. Sometimes licences are written in a way that makes it possible for the employees to use them at home.

7. *Employer's information*

Many people bring computers from their work to their home or they use their private computers to process their employer's information.

Advice: Never work with your employer's information on your private PC without their approval. If something goes wrong confidential information might be exposed to unauthorised people.

8. 'Illegal' information

Some information in databases might be considered as illegal. Examples are child pornography, threats against people, racist material etc.

Advice: If you come across this kind of information, contact your local police authority.

9. Anonymity on the Internet

Many people feel anonymous on the Internet. Especially if they are using Internet providers that claim they offer anonymity.

Advice: There are many ways to trace your identity. Be careful if you are giving away personal data on the Internet. You leave a lot of information everywhere. Do not do anything on the Internet that you cannot take responsibility for.

10. Back-up

At your office someone is allocated to, and responsible for, securing your data (making copies of all data, so called back-ups). At home you have to do it yourself.

Advice: Make copies of your user data on a regular basis. If you don't have access to back-up media for large volumes you can always make back-ups of your most important data files to a floppy disk. Standard software is normally possible to reload from other sources than your own back-up. However, a total back-up of the complete system is preferable. There are special storage devices available on the market for making backups. Save important data in two different places.

5

FUGITIVE INVESTIGATIVE SERVICES

One of the most important fields of activity of the global law enforcement community today is the apprehension of wanted persons.

Fugitives pose a serious threat to public safety worldwide. They are mobile and opportunistic; they frequently finance their continued flight from the law through further criminal activities, which may result in criminal charges in more than one country.

Fugitives also undermine the world's criminal justice systems. They may have been charged with a violation of the law but not been arrested. They may have been released on bail and then fled to avoid prosecution or, perhaps they have escaped from prison. When fugitives flee, cases are not adjudicated, convicted criminals fail to meet their obligations, and crime victims are denied justice.

INTERPOL'S ROLE

INTERPOL's activities in relation to international fugitives have been part of its core business since the organization's creation. INTERPOL circulates internationally, at the request of member countries, electronic diffusions and notices containing identification details and judicial information about wanted criminals.

The INTERPOL Red Notice has been recognised in a number of countries as having the legal value to serve as a basis for provisional arrest.

The persons concerned are wanted by national jurisdictions or International Criminal Tribunals, where appropriate, and the Red Notice is intended to help police identify or locate these individuals with a view to their arrest and extradition.

INTERPOL created the Fugitive Investigative Service to offer more proactive and systematic assistance to member countries by:

- providing investigative support to member countries in ongoing international fugitive investigations with a view to locating and arresting wanted persons;
- coordinating and enhancing international cooperation in the field of fugitive investigations;
- collecting and disseminating best practice and expert knowledge;
- conducting and coordinating relevant research and serve as a global point of reference for fugitive-related information.

PUBLIC SAFETY AND TERRORISM

Terrorism poses a grave threat to individuals' lives and national security around the world. INTERPOL has therefore made available various resources to support member countries in their efforts to protect their citizens from terrorism, including bio-terrorism; firearms and explosives; attacks against civil aviation; maritime piracy; and weapons of mass destruction.

INTERPOL collects, stores, analyses and exchanges information about suspected individuals and groups and their activities. The organization also co-ordinates the circulation of alerts and warnings on terrorists, dangerous criminals and weapons threats to police in member countries. A chief initiative in this area is the Fusion Task Force, which was created in the aftermath of the 11 September attacks in the United States.

In order to help member countries report terrorist activity, INTERPOL has issued practical guidelines on the type of information required.

Member countries are also encouraged to report on other crimes which may be linked to terrorism, such as suspicious financial transactions, weapons trafficking, money laundering, falsified travel and identity documents, and seizures of nuclear, chemical and biological materials.

The growing possibility of terrorists launching attacks with biological or chemical weapons is a particularly urgent concern. A dedicated bio-terrorism unit at the General Secretariat works to implement various projects with the close cooperation of INTERPOL National Central Bureaus and regional offices.

INTERPOL hosted two successful international bio-terrorism conferences in 2004 and 2005 which brought together hundreds of senior police officials and experts from specialised fields to share expertise and devise strategies to counter the threat.

TRAFFICKING IN HUMAN BEINGS

INTERPOL aims to end the abuse and exploitation of human beings for financial gain. Women from developing countries and young children all over the world are especially vulnerable to trafficking, smuggling or sexual exploitation.

Trafficking in women for sexual exploitation is a multi-billion-dollar business which involves citizens of most countries and helps sustain organized crime. A violation of human rights, it destroys the lives of its victims.

Human trafficking is distinct from people smuggling in that it involves the exploitation of the migrant, often for purposes of forced labour and prostitution.

People smuggling implies the procurement, for financial or material gain, of the illegal entry into a state of which that person is neither a citizen nor a permanent resident. Criminal networks which smuggle and traffic in human beings for financial gain increasingly control the flow of migrants across borders.

Child sexual exploitation on the Internet ranges from posed photos to visual recordings of brutal sexual crimes. One of INTERPOL's main tools for helping police fight this type of crime is the INTERPOL Child Abuse Image Database (ICAID).

Created in 2001, it contains hundreds of thousands of images of child sexual abuse submitted by member countries, thereby facilitating the sharing of images and information to assist law enforcement agencies with the identification of new victims.

CORRUPTION

'Working together towards a corruption-free world by promoting and defending integrity, justice and the rule of law'

MISSION STATEMENT OF THE INTERPOL ANTI-CORRUPTION ACADEMY

About Corruption

Corruption undermines political, social and economic stability. It threatens security and damages trust and public confidence in systems which affect people's daily lives. Although corruption frequently occurs at local or national level, its consequences are global; its hidden costs immense.

What is Corruption?

"Corruption undermines everything the law enforcement community works towards. It impoverishes whole communities, and threatens the safety and security of the many for the benefit of a very few" - INTERPOL Secretary General Ronald K. Noble

Corruption is a multifaceted phenomenon supported by differing historical and socio-economic conditions in each country. It exists at all levels of society.

Although in the past it could have been considered a largely domestic issue, corruption now often transcends national boundaries. Its consequences are global; its hidden costs immense.

The private sector has responded by implementing ethics and compliance standards and regulations, while the public sector benefits from the ratification of recent laws and international conventions. Oversight bodies and mechanisms have been created to ensure the smooth running of efforts in both sectors.

Nevertheless, corruption remains rampant in many countries, continuing to siphon off valuable resources and economic gains.

Why does Corruption Threaten good Governance?

Corruption is a manifestation of institutional weakness, poor ethical standards, skewed incentives and insufficient enforcement.

When corrupt officials slowly drain the resources of a country, its potential to develop socially and to attract foreign investment is diminished, making it incapable of providing basic services to or enforcing the rights of its citizens.

Furthermore, corruption fuels transnational crime. Terrorists and organized criminals could not carry out their illegal activities without the complicity of corrupt public officials.

It threatens security and damages trust in systems which affect people's daily lives. It is a particular concern for the world's police and judicial systems, as corruption in one country can compromise an entire international investigation.

Corruption itself does not produce poverty, but it does have a direct and immediate impact on economic growth and good governance, which in turn raises poverty levels. It remains a major obstacle to the achievement of the UN's eight Millennium Developments Goals, whose primary aim is to reduce poverty.

The most recent analyses indicate that corruption continues to thrive globally. But as the awareness of corruption increases, so too does the understanding of its negative effects on political, economic and social reforms.

Transparency International's 2006 report shows that corruption is rampant despite improved legislation and counter efforts.

More than US$1 trillion is paid in bribes alone each year, according to a World Bank Institute report - compared to the estimated size of the world economy at that time of just over US$30 trillion.

How do International Conventions Address the Problem?

Fighting corruption is challenging because the related offences are typically carried out in secret, while victims frequently realise it has occurred only after much time has passed. Although corruption can often be seen as purely a domestic issue, the international dimension of corruption is no less important, as corrupt acts usually take place in multiple places and are generally linked to crimes carried out in other countries.

The numerous existing conventions identify the current phenomenon of corruption as a matter of high concern. Definitions and academic approaches developed in the past years try to address the problem individually and collectively.

Although some of the conventions focus on one region, they all aim to fight corruption while emphasising the necessity of cooperation among countries.

International cooperation can help engender the will of countries to fight corruption and the capability to do so. Despite the obvious sensitivity of devising and implementing strategies to combat systematic corruption, international organizations can - and they already do - help by providing support for democratic reforms, more competitive economies and improved governance.

Even if virtually all forms of corruption are forbidden in most countries, some may face difficulties fighting it due to a lack of sufficient will or local capacity, such as proper strategies and structures, or funds.

Anti-corruption agreements constitute highly valuable tools for organizations, companies or citizens concerned with corruption and its impact on good governance. By establishing an international framework, the treaties can help foster a high-level of political commitment, suggest legal measures that countries could take and establish a programme of international and regional cooperation.

The United Nations Convention against Corruption (UNCAC) is one of the most important and recent steps in the global fight against corruption. The Convention went into force in December 2005 and has exceeded 140 signatories. It represents an important consensus about what countries should do in the areas of corruption prevention and criminalisation, as well as international cooperation and asset recovery.

The UNCAC is thus a milestone for the global effort to combat graft and provides a unique opportunity to build public awareness and commitment to curbing corruption.

INTERPOL AND CORRUPTION

As the world's largest international police organization, INTERPOL is taking its place at the forefront of the fight against corruption. Corruption is one of INTERPOL's six priority crime areas.

Fighting Corruption is a Priority for INTERPOL

INTERPOL has been actively involved in supporting initiatives to curb corruption since it hosted the First International Conference on Corruption-Related Crimes in 1998 at its General Secretariat in Lyon, France.

As the world's largest international police organization, INTERPOL is particularly concerned about the role corruption plays in terrorism and other international crimes.

The globalisation of crime in general makes it also necessary for law enforcement in different countries to work together to develop various means for fighting corruption.

INTERPOL established the INTERPOL Group of Experts on Corruption (IGEC) in 1998, and is currently in the process of developing the INTERPOL Anti-Corruption Office (IACO) and INTERPOL Anti-Corruption Academy (IACA).

These components support anti-corruption activities by establishing policies and standards, as well as conducting or assisting with education, research, training, investigations and asset-recovery operations. These initiatives are consistent with the United Nations Convention against Corruption, which entered into force on 15 December 2005, as well as the efforts of the United Nations Office on Drugs and Crime (UNODC) to strengthen the implementation of the Convention.

ADDITIONAL RESOURCES FOR ANTI-CORRUPTION PROFESSIONALS

INTERPOL has identified corruption as a priority crime area which warrants its full resources and efforts to fight it. The organization has embarked on a campaign to raise 15 million euros to create the world's first academic institute dedicated to the study, research and prevention of corruption.

In determining anti-corruption strategies and tactics, it is important to take into consideration the unique aspects of this crime.

The parties involved in perpetrating it all have an interest in keeping it secret. Because criminals are able to adapt quickly to new strategies developed by law enforcement, anti-corruption professionals also have to be dynamic and flexible, employing a holistic approach in cooperation with all major stakeholders.

INTERPOL's initiatives to date include:

- adoption of a Declaration of Intent for law enforcement during the INTERPOL General Assembly in Seoul, Korea, in 1999, encompassing a Code of Ethics and Code of Conduct for all law enforcement officers;
- collation of the Library of Best Practice designed to aid corruption investigators. Subjects include corruption strategies and structures, undercover investigations, operatives and techniques, witness

protection, anti-corruption legislation, prevention, training and education;

- formulation of Global Standards to Combat Corruption in Police Forces/Services, unanimously adopted by the INTERPOL General Assembly in Cameroon in September 2002, which promote high standards of honesty, integrity and ethics in the world's law enforcement agencies; provide a framework to improve their resistance to corruption; and promote the development in each member country of measures designed to prevent, detect and eradicate corruption. They contain principles and numerous measures designed to boost the efficiency of law enforcement in preventing corruption, as well as in the investigation of cases of corruption. The Standards are also commensurate with the spirit and content of the UN Convention against Corruption;
- a Police Integrity Survey to benchmark the capacities of INTERPOL's member countries to combat corruption. Follow-up surveys to track the progress are planned; and
- an international system of 'national contact points' through which law enforcement agencies in different countries can quickly initiate cooperation in corruption cases.

INTERPOL GROUP OF EXPERTS ON CORRUPTION (IGEC)

The INTERPOL Group of Experts on Corruption (IGEC) aims to develop and implement new initiatives to further law enforcement's efficiency in the fight against corruption. It is a multi-disciplinary group with members from all regions of the world, coordinating and harmonizing different national and regional approaches.

INTERPOL GROUP OF EXPERTS ON CORRUPTION (IGEC)

The INTERPOL Group of Experts on Corruption (IGEC), an outgrowth of the first International Conference on Corruption-related Crime, held at the INTERPOL General Secretariat in Lyon in April 1998, has been mandated by the INTERPOL General Assembly to develop and implement various new anti-corruption initiatives to further law enforcement's efficiency in the fight against corruption.

The IGEC is a multi-disciplinary group representing all of INTERPOL's regions which facilitates the coordination and harmonisation of the different national and regional approaches to combating corruption.

In addition, the group includes a host of other international stakeholders in the global anti-corruption campaign. The rationale underlying this structure is the general belief that law enforcement should combat corruption as a phenomenon holistically, in cooperation with all major players and the community at large.

IGEC's Membership and Eligibility

The IGEC has a comprehensive 'Terms of Reference' which clearly outlines all aspects relating to membership issues.

The IGEC is currently chaired by Mark Gough, Deputy Director, Investigations Division, Office of Internal Oversight Services at the United Nations, and is comprised of experts representing Austria, Australia, Canada, Egypt, Hong Kong (China), Malaysia, Mexico, Thailand, the United Kingdom and the United States, plus the European Commission, the Inter-American Development Bank, Transparency International, the University of Ottawa and the INTERPOL General Secretariat.

IGEC's Mission Statement

'We believe in a free and just society. To be truly just, society must embrace high standards of integrity and openly resist corruption.

To this end, we join with the community to ensure such standards and accept responsibility to fight all forms of corruption through education, prevention and effective law enforcement.'

Definition of Corruption

'Corruption is any course of action or failure to act by individuals or organizations, public or private, in violation of law or trust for profit or gain.'

IGEC's Role and Activities

The IGEC provides essential information and feedback to INTERPOL on matters pertaining to all aspects of corruption, and is mandated to advise the Secretary General on how best to combat this phenomenon, both operationally and strategically. In order to give effect to this mandate, the experts meet at least twice annually. The IGEC is present at all anti-corruption meetings and participates in most anti-corruption fora. It has also conducted numerous anti-corruption workshops and seminars and hosted several conferences. The group has established substantial credentials as being innovative and leading the fight against corruption globally.

The IGEC has a proven track record of success, with many accomplishments. It has conducted two 'Police Integrity Surveys' of INTERPOL's 186 member countries dealing with existing anti-corruption measures and their efficacy, with the objective of addressing and meeting the needs of member countries. In addition, in response to the results of the surveys, the IGEC has produced:

- a 'Declaration of Intent' for law enforcement, encompassing a 'Code of Ethics' and a 'Code of Conduct', which was subsequently adopted by the INTERPOL General Assembly in Seoul in 1999 (see AG Resolution)
- a draft set of 'Global Standards to Combat Corruption in Police Forces/Services,' which provide law enforcement with a framework to improve their resistance to corruption. They contain principles and numerous measures designed to improve the efficiency of law enforcement in preventing corruption, as well as in the investigation of cases of corruption. The objectives of the Global Standards are twofold:
- to ensure that the police forces/services in each INTERPOL member country demonstrate high standards of honesty, integrity and ethical behaviour in, and in connection with, the performance of their police functions;
- to promote and strengthen the development by each INTERPOL member country of measures needed to prevent, detect, punish and eradicate corruption in police forces/services within its national boundaries, and to bring to justice police officers and other employees of police forces/services who are corrupt. The measures address, for example:
- expected/ appropriate standards of conduct;
- effective recruitment;
- need for effective training;
- specific measures and systems aimed at the prevention - and reporting - of corruption.

The Global Standards included another first for INTERPOL: a provision authorising the INTERPOL General

Secretariat to monitor their implementation in member countries. The Global Standards are currently available in five languages - English, French, Spanish, Arabic and Chinese - and are accessible via INTERPOL's website.

- the collation of a 'Library of Best Practice,' designed to aid investigators in corruption cases. It covers a number of topics, including anti-corruption strategies and structures and their potential weaknesses, operatives and techniques in undercover investigations, witness protection, corruption legislation, prevention, training and education. This is available to law enforcement on CD and on INTERPOL'S restricted website, and to other stakeholders in the anti-corruption community by request. It should serve first and foremost as a reference or pointer system for organizations that actively lead the fight against corruption. For this reason, each contribution clearly states the source of the article. The reader will also find (attached as an appendix) a comprehensive list of agencies with an anti-corruption mandate and their contact details.

The 'Library of Best Practice' also serves to provide law enforcement officers with sufficient information on an array of important topics which should improve their ability and effectiveness in combating corruption. The objective of this tool is to facilitate the implementation and realisation of the 'Global Standards to Combat Corruption in Police Forces/ Services.'

IGEC's Contribution to the INTERPOL Anti-Corruption Academy

Having realised that its approach to training was not meeting the needs of the anti-corruption community, the IGEC deliberated further on this issue. The recognition by the IGEC of the need for a dedicated anti-corruption educational, training and research facility eventually led to the creation of the INTERPOL Anti-Corruption Academy.

The INTERPOL Anti-Corruption Academy

The INTERPOL Anti-Corruption Academy will be the world's first educational institute dedicated to fighting corruption. It will allow law enforcement professionals and other students to learn from the world's foremost authorities in anti-corruption training, research and investigation.

The INTERPOL Anti-Corruption Academy

The Anti-Corruption Academy will be a non-profit organization operated under the auspices of INTERPOL, and will work in conjunction with a special anti-corruption office established by INTERPOL (IACO), as well as a host of other strategic partners.

The Academy will be the world's first educational institute dedicated to fighting corruption.

Fully Equipped and Furnished Training Facility

INTERPOL wishes to recognise the extraordinary professional and personal commitment that Austria's government and late Minister of Interior Liese Prokop dedicated to making this dream for Austria and INTERPOL a reality.

The Austrian Government has agreed to provide state-of-the-art infrastructure for the Academy, which includes accommodation and catering facilities. The proposed building, part of an elegant 16th-century convent, will provide the ideal setting and ambiance for an institute of higher learning of this nature. The building will be adapted to include lecture and computer rooms, accommodation, dining facilities and a study area.

Real-world Curriculum

Internationally recognized scholars, practitioners and prominent academics will be engaged by the Academy to ensure that it becomes the most innovative global provider of anti-corruption education, training, investigative assistance, and research.

Furthermore, especially to meet the need in developing countries to undertake more complex investigations, the Academy will become a forum to express and exchange innovative ideas to confront the most vexing problems facing the global law enforcement community.

The curriculum, developed by experienced educators and corruption experts, will be the key to the Academy's success. Topics will include oversight and investigation of high-profile corruption cases, independent agency creation and management, forensic accounting, ethics, asset tracing and recovery, money laundering, and computer-based evidence gathering.

Courses will comprise a set of modules on different subjects which can be taken individually or combined, and typical sessions may last from one week to three months. Coursework, both practical and theoretical, will offer real case studies reflecting the laws, cultures and capabilities of different countries.

The Academy will seek official accreditation by negotiating agreements with recognized universities to allow its graduates to apply their course credits toward university degrees in fields such as law and criminal justice.

Research will also be an important priority of the Academy.

Education will be achieved not only through courses but also through conferences, seminars and workshops and the Academy will serve as a think tank and will have the capacity and capability to undertake research assignments for other organisations, subject to funding, and will promote cooperation and collaboration within the anti-corruption community.

Additionally, it is INTERPOL's strategy to expand the Academy to include regional academies, using already established training centres in Asia, the Americas, Africa, and the Pacific regions, to cater for language, cultural and regional differences, and to reduce costs to students and faculties.

The proposal for an INTERPOL Anti-Corruption Academy is also consistent with numerous articles set out in the UN Convention against Corruption, which entered into force with effect from 15 December 2005, as well as other anti-corruption conventions and treaties, and supports the efforts of the United Nations Office on Drugs and Crime (UNODC) to strengthen the implementation of the Convention.

Renowned Faculty

The Academy will employ full-time professors and researchers with advanced academic credentials, and select guest lecturers and senior practitioners of renown to supplement this expertise.

As well as providing quality education, research and methodology, this will offer students maximum exposure to multilingual, culturally diverse experts from academia, government, the business community, non-governmental organizations, development agencies and international financial institutions.

Governance Structure

The Academy's day-to-day management will be effected by a dean. The governance structure of the Academy is expected to include an oversight body to ensure that high standards of education, management, policy and accountability are maintained. The composition and role of this governing body are currently being developed.

In order to achieve the below-mentioned strategic aims, an Academic Project Management Committee was appointed at the beginning of 2007, composed of experts from academia from all over the world.

Together, with experts from INTERPOL, the Committee will formulate recommendations on different aspects related to education, training, research and governance of the Academy.

Strategic Aims

By contributing to the Academy, donors will be helping to create the world's first international centre of excellence dedicated to rooting out corrupt practices at all levels of society. Over time, the Academy will be able to expand its reach beyond education and research to include:

- Assistance with the implementation of the United Nations Convention against Corruption (UNCAC), and other international conventions;
- Training and deployment of anti-corruption professionals at the national level;
- Creation of an international anti-corruption network; and
- Assurance of international good practice and uniform standards in prevention, detection and prosecution of corruption.

Ultimately this will lead to increased transparency in the public and private sector, thereby restoring public confidence in its institutions.

The private sector, particularly large multinationals, will

see lower costs and less waste. Other international organizations and non-governmental bodies will have an invaluable partner in their efforts to foster stable and just societies.

Legal agreements signed between the Austrian Government and INTERPOL set out further provisions. In terms of accountability, INTERPOL will carry out annual internal and external audits, and will be subject to regular reporting on the Academy, to its Executive Committee and General Assembly.

The strategic aims of the Academy are:

- to professionalize anti-corruption work, and exchange practices and standards in jurisdictions globally; and
- to improve the efficiency and efficacy of all those agencies, entities, or individuals throughout the world, whose primary function is to prevent, detect, or prosecute corruption.

The Academy will affect the above-mentioned objectives through:

- Development of original, curricula, based on the insights of Academy faculty, and other anti-corruption experts and staff;
- Ongoing education for a growing cadre of anti-corruption professionals, using e-learning as a substantial support mechanism;
- Recruitment of guest lecturers and instructors with extensive practical experience to augment and enhance the baseline curricula to enable the Academy to maintain a critical mass of expertise in the subject areas, and allow for a continuous source of fresh insights and information;

- Development of a feedback loop between alumni of the Academy and Academy faculty to ensure that the practical lessons alumni learn within their respective countries will be incorporated into future Programs;
- Establishment of innovative research programs in coordination with other international bodies and research universities, to provide vital information to countries and international organizations on effective anti-corruption strategies. This research program will instil a culture of continuous innovation in anti-corruption practices globally;
- Participation in standard-setting groups and other global anti-corruption organizations to enable the Academy to extend its influence in practical, everyday applications; and
- Collaboration with colleges and universities to professionalize anti-corruption work, especially related to implementation of various treaties like the United Nations Convention Against Corruption, as well as providing country specific investigative assistance and information sharing.

Funding Goals and Fundraising

In an important first step, the Austrian government has generously agreed to provide:

- a fully equipped and furnished state of the art education, training and research facility; and
- a conference to introduce the Academy to decision makers both in the public and private sectors.

The Academy will function as a non-profit, organization, and contributions will be tax-deductible in the majority of our member countries.

Initial start-up funding totalling 15 million euros, is currently being raised to facilitate three years' operational costs, after which it aims to become self-sustaining through revenue from student fees, donations, research contracts and ancillary services, such as publication sales, conference attendance fees and short-term executive education.

To ensure the Academy is accessible to all, financial assistance - from international organizations, governments, development agencies and the private sector - will be sought to support the participation of students from less-developed countries.

Further information will soon be provided by the project manager to the public and private sectors, as well as further details on the potential for tax deductions.

PARTNERSHIPS

Details of law enforcement and agencies who are partners in the fight against corruption.

List of international, regional and non-governmental agencies International, Regional and NGO.

Name

Anti-corruption gateway for Europe and Eurasia

Address

CEE Program Officer, Criminal Law Reform Program

740 15th Street, NW

Washington, DC 20005 USA

Email : NoBribes@abaceeli.org

Contact : Jennifer Gauck - Deputy Program Coordinator, Anti-Corruption

Description : The Anti-Corruption Gateway for Europe

and Eurasia is a significant entrance way to information about combating corruption. It offers primary materials and direct links to major information sources for anti-corruption practitioners and analysts engaged in Eastern Europe and the Former Soviet Union.

Name

Anti-Corruption Network for Transition Economies

Address

Secretariat of the Anti-Corruption Network

Anti-Corruption Division

Directorate for Financial and Enterprise Affairs Organisation for Economic Cooperation and Development (OECD)

2, Rue André-Pascal

75775 Paris Cedex 16 France

Telephone: + 33 (0) 1 45 24 91 06

Email : Anti-Corruption.Network@oecd.org

Website:www.oecd.org/pages/0,2966,en_36595778_36595861_1_1_1_1_1,00.html

Description: The Anti-Corruption Network for Transition Economies (ACN) is a regional anti-corruption initiative that was established in 1998 by national governments, civil society organisations, and international donor agencies to promote knowledge sharing, donor coordination and policy dialogue in the transition economies in Central, Eastern, and South Eastern Europe and the Newly Independent States.

The main objective of the ACN is to assist the participating countries to strengthen their capacity to tackle anti-corruption reform and to move closer to international standards.

Within OECD:

Anti-Corruption Network for Transition Economies (ACN)

Support for Improvement in Governance and Management (SIGMA Programme)

Public Governance and Management (PUMA)

Financial Action Task Force on Money

Name

African Parliamentarians' Network Against Corruption

Address

Hon Augustine Ruzindana

NHIF Building

3rd Floor

P.O. Box 9023-00200

Nairobi , Kenya

Telephone: (+ 254) (0) 20 2738142/3

Email : apnacsecretariat@yahoo.com

augustine@starcom.co.ug

Contact

Interim secretariat:

Charity Wakaba

Parliamentary Centre

255 Albert Street Suite 802

Ottawa , ON K1P 6A9

Canada

Tel : 613 - 237 0143

Email: secretariat@apnacafrica.org

Website : www.apnacafrica.org

Description: Africa's leading network of parliamentarians working to strengthen parliamentary capacity to fight corruption and promote good governance.

Name

The Asian Development Bank Anti-corruption unit

Address Headquarters

6 ADB Avenue

Mandaluyong City 1550

Philippines

Mailing Address

P.O. Box 789

0980 Manila

Philippines

Telephone HQ: + 632 632 4444

Email : information@adb.org

Website : www.adb.org/Anticorruption/unit.asp

Name

Asia Crime Prevention Foundations

Address

5th floor Sumitomo Higushi-Shinbashi

Bldg No. 3 1-10-14

Hamamatsu-cho

Minato-Ku Tokyo 105-0013

Japan

Telephone: +81-3-3433-2124

Email : info@acpf.org

Website : www.acpf.org/index(E).htm

Description: ACPF is an international non-governmental organization, established in 1982, to promote sustainable development, peace and stability in Asia and the world through more effective crime prevention, criminal justice policies and practices, and mutual cooperation among all those concerned.

Name

Centre for International Private Enterprise Anti-Corruption Program

Address

1155 15th Street NW

Suite 700

Washington, DC 20005

USA

Telephone : +1 202 721-9200

Website:www.cipe.org/programs/corruption/index.htm

Description : CIPE's anti-corruption work targets both the supply and demand sides of corruption.

On the supply side, CIPE and its partner organizations address private sector participation in corruption by working to create an environment where corrupt activities become unsustainable.

This can be achieved in large part by building and improving corporate governance mechanisms.

On the demand side, CIPE's programs seek to reform ambiguous legal systems, implement standards for government agencies, make a link between cultural norms and rule of law, and change laws to mitigate government employees' opportunities to exert discretionary (and unsupervised) authority throughout various levels of government.

Name

Centro Latinoamericano de Administración para el Desarrollo (CLAD) - Red de Instituciones de Combate a la Corrupción y Rescate de la Ética Pública, RICOREP

Address

Centro Latinoamericano de Administración para el Desarrollo (CLAD)

Calle Herrera Toro, Quinta CLAD, Sector Los Naranjos, Las Mercedes

Apartado Postal 4181. Caracas 1010-A

Venezuela

Telephone : (58-212) 9924064/3297/5953/9937277/9104

Email : clad@clad.org.ve

clad@reacciun.ve

Website : www.clad.org.ve

Description : RICOREP brings together government and non-government organizations which have the purpose of fighting corruption in all its forms and to draw principles of ethics for the exercise of public functioning. RED also works with people who develop studies and investigations.

Name

European Anti-Fraud Office - OLAF

Address (mail)

OLAF

European Commission

B -1049 Brussels

Belgium

Address (office)

rue Joseph II, 30

1000 Brussels

Belgium

Telephone (general) : +32-2-296.08.53

Email (general) : olaf-courrier@ec.europa.eu

Website: http://ec.europa.eu/anti_fraud/index_en.html

Name

European Healthcare Fraud and Corruption Network

Address

158 Avenue de Tervueren

1150 Brussels

Belgium

Tel: +32 2 739 7507

Fax: +32 2 7397901

Email : enquiries@ehfcn.org

Contact

Marleen De Wulf

EHFCN Office

Website : www.ehfcn.org

Description: To coordinate and advance work to counter healthcare fraud and corruption, the Network has been formally established and an Office has been set-up, which is dedicated to tackling healthcare fraud and corruption across Europe.

The Office is a not-for-profit organisation, based in Brussels and financed through subscription fees.

Name

European Partners against Corruption - EU's national police monitoring and inspection bodies and anti-corruption agencies

Address

c/o BIA - Federal Bureau for Internal Affairs

Austrian Federal Ministry of the Interior

Herrengasse 7, A-1014 Wien, Austria

Telephone: +43-(0)-1-531 26 -0

Website : www.epac.at

Description: Catalogue with national bureaus for investigating corruption matters can be found on the website.

Name

Global Organisation of Parliamentarians against corruption (updated 18.09.07)

Address

255 Albert Street, Suite 802

Ottawa, Ontario K1P 6A9, Canada

Telephone : + :1 613 432 1640 ; 1 613 237 0143 X 371

Email : Campbell.Meaghan@gmail.com ;

info@gopacnetwork.org

Website : www.gopacnetwork.org

Description: Contact persons :

Meaghan Campbell

Communications and Program(s) Consultant

Kimberley Jordan

Program(s) Assistant

The Global Organization Against Corruption (GOPAC) is an international network of parliamentarians dedicated to good governance and combating corruption throughout the world.

Name

Global Witness

Address

Global Witness

PO Box 6042

London N19 5WP, UK

Telephone : +44 (0)20 7272 6731

Email : mail@globalwitness.org

Website : www.globalwitness.org/index.php

Description : Global Witness was the first organization that sought to break the links between the exploitation of natural resources, and conflict and corruption. Global Witness exposes the corrupt exploitation of natural resources and international trade systems, to drive campaigns that end impunity, resource-linked conflict, and human rights and environmental abuses. Relevant areas of work are corruption in oil, gas and mining as well as the role of financial institutions.

Name

Group of States against Corruption (GRECO) - Council of Europe

Address

Avenue de l'Europe

67075 Strasbourg Cedex

France

Telephone : +33 (0)3 88 41 30 43

Email : webmaster.greco@coe.int

Contact

Mr Wolfgang RAU - Executive Secretary

Website : www.coe.int

Description : According to its Statute, the aim of the GRECO is to improve its members' capacity to fight corruption by monitoring the compliance of States with their undertakings in this field. In this way, it will contribute to identifying deficiencies and insufficiencies of national mechanisms against corruption, and to prompting the necessary legislative, institutional and practical reforms in order to better prevent and combat corruption.

The Council of Europe also undertook another short term anti-corruption project called PACO - impact project for the implementation of anti-corruption plans in South-eastern Europe. This program terminated July 2006

Name

Indonesia Corruption Watch

Address

Jl. Kalibata Timur IV/D

No. 6 Jakarta Selatan

Indonesia

Telephone : +62 - 21 - 7901 885, 7994 015

Email : icw@antikorupsi.org.

Website : www.antikorupsi.org/eng/

Description : Indonesia Corruption Watch (ICW) was established on 21 June 1998 in the middle of reform movements that demanded for clean government, which free from corruption, collusion and nepotism

Name

IFES - Democracy and governance assistance organization

Address

1101 15th Street NW ,

Third Floor, Washington,

D.C. 20005

Telephone: +1 202 350 6700

Website : http://www.ifes.org/

Other: In its Governance program IFES helps to improve the transparency and efficiency of government institutions by building the management capacity, independence and professionalism of public officials in order to enable them to better serve their constituents.

Name

International Association of Prosecutors

Address

Hartogstraat 13

2514 EP

The Hague

The Netherlands

Telephone: +31 70 3630345/52

Email : sg@iap.nl.com

info@iap.nl.com

Website : www.iap.nl.com/

Description: The International Association of Prosecutors (IAP) is a non-governmental and non-political organization. Its creation was in response to the rapid growth in serious transnational crime, particularly drug trafficking, money laundering and fraud. There was a perceived need for greater international cooperation between prosecutors and for faster and more efficient mutual assistance, asset tracking and other international co-operative measures.

Name

The International Budget Project

Address

International Budget Project of the Centre on Budget and Policy Priorities

820 First Street, NE Suite 510

Washington, DC 20002, USA

Telephone : +1 202 408 1080

Email : info@internationalbudget.org

Website : www.internationalbudget.org/index.htm

Description : The International Budget Project was formed within the Centre on Budget and Policy Priorities in 1997 to nurture the growth of civil society capacity to analyze and influence government budget processes, institutions and outcomes. The overarching aim of the project is to make budget systems more responsive to the needs of society and, accordingly, to make these systems more transparent and accountable to the public.

Name

International Centre for Asset Recovery (ICAR)

Address

Basel Institute on Governance

Peter Merian-Weg 8

P.O. Box

CH-4002 Basel

Telephone : Phone +41 (0)61 267 05 00

Fax +41 (0)61 267 24 81

Email : info@baselgovernance.org

Website : http://www.baselgovernance.org/icar/

Other : ICAR specializes in training and assisting developing countries on the practical work of tracing, confiscating and repatriating the proceeds of corruption, money laundering and related crimes. ICAR assists developing countries in building capacities and setting up necessary procedures and institutions to more effectively make use of international legal assistance in criminal matters for the purpose of recovering stolen assets.

Name

International Compliance Association

Address

ICA Registrar

International Compliance Association

Wrens Court

52-54 Victoria Road

Sutton Coldfield

Birmingham B72 1SX

UK

Telephone

Training and Courses (+44) (0) 121 362 7501

ICA membership (+44) (0) 121 362 7747

Email : Training and Courses ict@int-comp.com

ICA membership ica@int-comp.org

Website : www.int-comp.org/

Other : The ICA is a professional organisation dedicated to the furtherance of best compliance and anti money laundering practice in the financial services sector.

Name

International Group for anti-corruption coordination

Address

Global Programme against Corruption

UN Office on Drugs and Crime

Vienna International Centre

P.O. Box 500 , Room E1482

A-1400 Vienna

Austria

Telephone : +43(1)26060-4372

Website : www.igac.net/

Description : The International Group for Anti-Corruption Coordination (IGAC) is dedicated to strengthening international anti-corruption coordination and collaboration in order to avoid undue duplication and to ensure effective and efficient use of existing resources, using systems already in place at the regional and national level.

Name

Partnership for Transparency Fund

Address

4355 Klingle St NW

Washington DC 20016

USA

Email : ptf@partnershipfortransparency.info

Website : www.partnershipfortransparency.info/

Description : PTF is an international non-governmental organization dedicated to helping civil society play an effective role in the design, implementation and monitoring of national anti-corruption programs.

Name

Stability Pact Anti-corruption Initiative

Address

Mailing Address

Bistrik 5, 71000, Sarajevo

Bosnia and Herzegovina

Telephone : +387 33 550 220

Email : Executive Secretary

Mr. Veselin Sukovic

Email: sukovicv@lol.ba

Anti-Corruption Expert

Mr. Cornel - Virgiliu Calinescu

Email: calinescucv@lol.ba

Administrative Assistant

Ms. Dajana Stajic

Email: stajicd@lol.ba

Website : http://spai-rslo.org/new.asp

Description : The Stability Pact Anti-Corruption Initiative (SPAI) intends to give an impetus to the fight against corruption in the region by building upon existing actions through better coordination of all efforts and by relying on high-level political commitment.

Name

Support for Improvement in Governance and Management (SIGMA Programme)

Address

Located in OECD

Website : www.sigmaweb.org

Description: Sigma is a joint initiative of the OECD andthe European Union, principally financed by the EU. In 1992 the European Commission (EC) and the Organisation for Economic Cooperation and Development (OECD) launched the Sigma Programme to help countries in Central and Eastern Europe modernise their public governance systems. Principally financed by the European Union, Sigma supports candidate country administrations in their preparations for successful entry into the EU. Since July 2001 Sigma has also assisted countries in the Western Balkans in building legal and institutional frameworks that promote good governance and management. The Sigma Programme is also an integral part of the OECD's Centre for Cooperation with Non-Members (CCNM).

Name

Tiri

Address

Head Office

3rd floor Downstream Building

1 London Bridge

London SE1 9BG

Telephone: + 44-20-7022 1905

Email : info@tiri.org

Website : www.tiri.org/

Other: Tiri aims to raise integrity standards in specified institutions around the world. We seek to achieve this by facilitating a growing global network of reform leaders, specialists, and policy practitioners informed by objective and reliable evidence.

Name

Transnational Crime and Corruption Centre

(updated 17.09.07)

Address

Transnational Crime and Corruption Centre

American University

School of Public Policy,

George Mason University

3401 Fairfax Drive, MS 3B1

Arlington, VA 22201, USA

Ph: (703) 993-9757

Fax: (703) 993-8193

http://policy-traccc.gmu.edu

Email : traccc@american.edu; lshelley@gmu.edu

Website : www.american.edu/traccc/

Description : The Transnational Crime and Corruption Centre (TraCCC) is the first centre in the United States devoted to teaching, research, training and formulating policy advice in transnational crime, corruption and terrorism.

TraCCC's fundamental goal is to better understand the causes and scope of transnational crime and corruption and to propose well-grounded policy to reduce and eliminate these problems.

Name

Transparency International

Address

Alt Moabit 96

10559 Berlin

Germany

Telephone : +49-30-34 38 20-0

Email : ti@transparency.org

Website : www.transparency.org

Name

United Nations Office of Drugs and Crime

Global Programme Against Corruption

Address

Vienna International Centre

P.O. Box 500,

Room E1480,

A-1400 Vienna

Austria

Telephone: +43(1) 26060-5017

Email : anti-corruption@unodc.org

Website : www.unodc.org/unodc/corruption.html

Description: The Global Programme against Corruption (GPAC) is a catalyst and a resource to help countries effectively implement the provision of the UN Convention against Corruption. The primary goal of the Anti-Corruption Unit (ACU)/Global Programme against Corruption (GPAC) is to provide practical assistance and build technical capacity to implement the UNCAC and efforts will concentrate on supporting Member States in the development of anti-corruption policies and institutions. This will include the establishment of preventive anti-corruption frameworks.

Name

World Bank - Governance and Anti-corruption

Address (headquarter)

1818 H Street, NW

Washington, DC 20433 USA

Telephone (general) : +1 202-473-1000

Email : askgov@worldbank.org

Website : www.worldbank.org/wbi/governance

Description : Hundreds of governance and anti-corruption activities are taking place throughout the World Bank Group focusing on internal organizational integrity, minimizing corruption on World Bank-funded projects, and assisting countries in improving governance and controlling corruption.

CALENDAR OF EVENTS

The objective of this calendar is to provide the anti-corruption Community with an easy-to-access central reference point to events promoting the combating of Corruption.

The objective of this calendar is to facilitate :

1. greater awareness of anti-corruption events worldwide;
2. better planning and coordination of new events to avoid unnecessary duplication

Readers are encouraged to inform the INTERPOL General Secretariat at the below-mentioned e-mail address, of any conferences, meetings, discussion fora, workshops or other relevant events, so that this calendar may be kept up-to-date.

Currently, this table is not exhaustive.

INTERPOL'S OTHER AREAS OF CRIME

While not considered priority crime areas within the organization's current operational framework, other issues of concern for law enforcement in which Interpol remains active are:

- Genocide, war crimes and crimes against humanity
- Environmental crime
- Law enforcement corruption.

Interpol supports member countries and ad-hoc International Criminal Tribunals in the location and apprehension of criminals wanted for genocide, war crimes and crimes against humanity, primarily through the organization of working group meetings and conferences, publication of Red Notices and provision of other investigative assistance.

Environmental crime is a serious and growing international problem, with criminals violating national and international laws put in place to protect the environment. In the pursuit of financial gain, criminals are polluting the world's natural resources and pushing commercially valuable wildlife species closer to extinction, thereby significantly impacting the biological integrity of the planet.

With the goal of improving the quality of police forces and the services they provide, Interpol works with law enforcement around the world to help ensure that police officials, as civic leaders and role models, remain faithful to the tenets of their profession.

The organization has undertaken the task of developing and implementing an anti-corruption strategy, with the objective of not only raising awareness of the major issues, but also enhancing law enforcement's ability and effectiveness to fight law enforcement corruption.

6

Genocide, War Crimes, and Crimes Against Humanity

The Investigation and Prosecution of Genocide

The General Secretariat is expanding its role in providing international coordination and support for law enforcement agencies in member countries and international organizations responsible for the investigation and prosecution of genocide, war crimes, and crimes against humanity.

Interpol has been supporting member countries and the ad hoc International Criminal Tribunals in the location and apprehension of criminals wanted for genocide, war crimes, and crimes against humanity since 1994, primarily through the publication of Red Notices and the provision of other investigative assistance.

However, many countries have recently expanded their activities in this field, and have established specialized units dedicated to the investigation and prosecution of these offences regardless of where they have occurred.

From 23 to 25 March 2004, General Secretariat hosted the First International Expert Meeting on War Crimes, Genocide, and Crimes Against Humanity in Lyon, France. Ninety three delegates and observers from 39 countries and international organizations attended this meeting. Over the course of three days, the delegates viewed presentations and participated in discussions aimed at identifying the needs of the member countries and international organizations with a view towards improving coordination and information sharing. At the conclusion of the meeting, a list of recommendations was adopted.

From 21 to 22 July 2004, in furtherance of Recommendation no 9 adopted at the expert meeting, the General Secretariat hosted the First Working Group Meeting on Genocide, War Crimes, and Crimes Against Humanity, in Lyon.

Fourteen delegates from twelve countries and two international organizations participated in the discussions and made recommendations concerning ways to address the needs identified at the expert meeting.

The recommendations included the increased use of Interpol databases, the preparation of a best practice manual, and identification of points of contact in member countries.

On 7 October 2004, the General Assembly adopted Resolution number AG-2004-PRES-17 which recommended that, within the limits of national and international law, ICPO-Interpol member countries should cooperate with each other and with international organizations, international criminal tribunals, and non-governmental organizations as appropriate in a joint effort to prevent genocide, war crimes, and crimes against humanity, and to investigate and prosecute those suspected of committing these crimes; asked the General Secretariat to assist member countries in the investigation and prosecution of these crimes; and asked the Secretary General to bring the present resolution to the attention of the appropriate United Nations authorities and other international organizations.

The General Assembly Delegates also authorized an accord to be signed with the Office of the Prosecutor of the

International Criminal Court to improve cooperation between the two organizations in assisting the fight against transnational crime and upholding justice. The agreement will also allow the International Criminal Court access to Interpol's communications network and databases.

From 23 to 24 February 2005 the General Secretariat hosted the Second Working Group Meeting on Genocide, War Crimes, and Crimes Against Humanity, in Lyon. Eighteen delegates from thirteen countries and three international organizations participated.

The working group continued its work from the first meeting in July 2004 concerning improvement of information sharing and coordination of activities among member countries with regard to the investigation and prosecution of genocide, war crimes, and crimes against humanity.

From 14 to 16 June 2005 ICPO-Interpol hosted the Second International Expert Meeting on Genocide, War Crimes, and Crimes Against Humanity.

The purpose of this 2nd expert meeting was to share information concerning the activities of units and organizations specialised in these types of investigations, to discuss ways in which the needs of these units and organizations can be fulfilled, and to enhance the cooperation among the many law enforcement, judicial, academic, and non-governmental organizations involved in this complex field.

The three-day conference included presentations on various countries' war crimes programs and policies, the prosecution of Nazi war criminals, child soldiers, forensic science applications, human rights and international cooperation. There were also panel discussions on witness protection and international law and the role of non-governmental organizations in the investigation of genocide, war crimes and crimes against humanity.

ENVIRONMENTAL CRIME

Environmental crime is a serious and growing international problem, with criminals violating national and international laws put in place to protect the environment. These criminals are polluting the air, water and land. They are pushing commercially valuable wildlife species closer to extinction and they are significantly impacting the biological integrity of the planet.

Beginning in 1992, Interpol became actively involved in fighting environmental crime. Its programme has grown significantly over the years and continues to expand as member countries become more active in Interpol's two working groups. Each working group is headed by a specialised police officer with extensive experience in the field. Also :

25/09/2007 Fighting wildlife crime is focus of working group meeting in Tanzania

14/06/2007 Cover letter for Advocacy Memorandum

14/06/2007 Advocacy memorandum - Arguments for Prosecutors of Environmental Crimes

13/06/2006 Pollution Crimes Working Group, 5-6 June 2007, Lyon, France - Meeting minutes

14/02/2007 Paris MOU press release - Concentrated Inspection Campaign on MARPOL Annex I

06/06/2006 Interpol Pollution Crimes Working Group - Assessing the Links between Organised Crime and Pollution Crimes

22/03/2006 Training for Kenya Wildlife Service

03/06/2005 Interpol environmental crime conference calls for more international cooperation. Appointment of Interpol's first specialised officer in wildlife crimes announced

REGIONAL ACTIVITIES

Mission Statement

With a view to supporting INTERPOL's core functions and activities, the Directorate will focus its activities on three main areas:

- I-24/7 development, with the aim of maintaining and improving an operational, secure communications system between the General Secretariat and the NCBs, and to ensure and develop direct, immediate access to police information in INTERPOL's databases by national police services
- Capacity building, with the aim of developing and enhancing close cooperation with the N CBs in order to enhance their operational capacities and responsiveness
- Police training, with the aim of strengthening NCB staff's abilities in INTERPOL's core functions and their knowledge of INTERPOL's tools and services, and to increase awareness of INTERPOL within national law enforcement departments

Detailed description of activities

I-24/7 development

- Ensure INTERPOL maintains and enhances its leadership in global police communications and meets the international police cooperation expectations of its member countries by working in close collaboration with the National Central Bureaus
- Supervise the coordination of all organizational activities related to the maintenance and support of the I-24/7 global police communications system, including remote access to INTERPOL's databases

through integrated solutions (FIND/MIND), mobile access and others

- Help promote use of the databases and data services-based on the requirements of the member countries-by conducting appropriate activities, and to develop new data services according member countries' needs
- Continuously assess the levels of data management in the N CBs and recommend initiatives and steps needed to increase the level; assess the resources available and needed, as well as the training required, to optimize use of the databases and data services
- Implement externally-funded technical projects linked to the development of INTERPOL's global police communications system
- Ensure I-24/7 security standards at the General Secretariat and at user level
- Organize the INTERPOL Law Enforcement Technology Advisory Group.

Capacity Building

- Assist member countries with the creation and reconstruction of NCBs, revitalizing their operational capacities
- Maintain and develop N CB service standards and to promote good practice in all areas of police activities.
- Develop contact officers networks in order to enhance operational support between NCBs
- Produce the regional business plans in close cooperation with the relevant departments of the General Secretariat and the member countries
- Organize the annual Heads of NCBs meetings and the Regional Conferences

- Respond as quickly as possible to inquiries from N CBs addressed to the General Secretariat, and intervene on behalf of NCBs having difficulty obtaining responses from other NCBs
- Develop cooperation with regional and international organizations
- Support the activities of the Command and Coordination Centre when requested, on a case-by-case basis, by liaising with the member countries.
- Serve as a link between N CBs and people responsible for crime support programmes and projects at the General Secretariat

Police Training

- Carry out tailored I-24/7 user training courses worldwide according national needs
- Organize NCB staff training courses for national officers working at INTERPOL National Central Bureaus on a regional and language basis
- Organize INTERPOL awareness seminars at the request of member countries
- Inform crime programme managers of training requirements in their area

EXCHANGE OF GOOD PRACTICE BETWEEN NCBS

Activity

After the 17 service standards had been adopted at the 63rd General Assembly session held in Rome in 1994, member countries suggested a mechanism for implementing the service. The European region adopted a peer evaluation mechanism in 1999 in order to implement the service standards.

The evaluation yielded a number of positive results ranging from enhanced status of the NCBs to the allocation of additional resources. Discussion with member countries during many INTERPOL meetings on the European mechanism has generated strong support.

It is against this background that it was decided to extend the exchange of good practice between NCBs to other regions based on different processes to be adopted for each region. The exchange of good practice programme began with a pilot scheme in 2004 in which volunteer N CBs were requested to participate in the exchange of best practice, and the scheme is being fully implemented in all INTERPOL regions. All INTERPOL's NCBs will have been visited before the end of 2009.

Objectives

The Exchange of Good Practice Programme is aimed at enhancing the status and role of NCBs and increasing countries' contribution to and use of the General Secretariat's databases.

- Ensure NCBs observe the minimum service standards required for their effective operation
- Enhance the status of NCBs
- Obtain additional resources for NCBs

Outcome

Based on the recommendations produced by the good practice teams and the good practice identified in the countries visited, we intend to increase the resources of our NCBs, to enhance their position within their national police structures and to meet the INTERPOL Services Standards required in order to provide a minimum of services to the international police community. When necessary, INTERPOL also provides equipment to those NCBs which lack resources.

CONTACT OFFICERS NETWORKS

Activity

The work performed by the network of contact officers throughout the world has resulted in many urgent cases being solved by our member countries.

In 2006, contact officers network meetings were organized in Europe, Africa, Asia and the South Pacific and the Middle East and North Africa, with participants from a total of 57 countries.

Objectives

The contact officers' network has been created to facilitate immediate assistance between NCBs in urgent cases.

Outcome

Details, names and telephone numbers of contact officers for Africa, Asia, Europe, and the Americas are now posted on the INTERPOL dashboard for the use of all NCBs.

NCB STAFF TRAINING

Activity

The NCB staff training courses organized by the NCB & I-24/7 Directorate were carried out aimed at improving the ability of the officers to perform their duties satisfactorily with regard to the requirements of international police cooperation and the range of services developed at INTERPOL.

Objectives

The main objective is to identify needs and assist in the implementation of NCB training programmes, co-or dinate member countries' training needs and ensure new and existing NCB staff are well informed and fully aware of:

- INTERPOL's services
- the role and function of NCBs
- INTERPOL policy in relation to international police cooperation

Outcome

The positive result of the training courses is the improvement in the quality and volume of messages most of our N CBs are now exchanging. This is clear from the increase in the amount of data entered in the INTERPOL database and increased use of the database.

INTERPOL AWARENESS SEMINARS

Activity

A seminar consists of a one or two-day general programme with presentations on INTERPOL's goals, structure and role, I-24/7 secure global police communications services (Dashboard, expansion, etc.), operational databases, crime programmes and projects, operational support provided by INTERPOL to major international events and incidents, structure and role of the NCB and key activities at national level.

An INTERPOL Awareness Seminar is generally organized in a country at the request of the NCB concerned.

The NCB defines the contents of the seminar in close cooperation with the General Secretariat, and is responsible for inviting representatives from national law enforcement agencies, customs and immigration at different levels (managers, operational units, specialized units, etc.).

This activity can equally be applied to international police academies worldwide as part of their regular training curricula.

Objectives

The aim of this activity is to increase national knowledge of INTERPOL's core functions and activities to:

- enhance the position of the NCB at national level and, consequently, obtain more support and resources for it;
- convince the national police community of the advantage of expanding the I-24/7 network and its contents beyond the NCB as an indispensable tool, not only for the NCB, but also for control, investigative and analytical units within national police forces;
- promote the use of INTERPOL's databases and services by the NCB, law enforcement agencies, customs, immigration services, investigative units, etc.

Outcome

Greater awareness of INTERPOL's services by national law enforcement departments leads to an immediate increase in the use of the NCBs by the national police community, which directly impacts the volume and efficiency of information exchange at national and international level.

INTERNATIONAL LIAISON

INTERPOL seeks to forge ties with all international bodies, governmental authorities and non-governmental organizations whose mission to fight crime and protect the public's safety.

These collaborations occur formally, through the signing of cooperation agreements and adoption of international conventions, and more informally, through INTERPOL's participation in international symposia, conferences and working groups, and vice versa. The aims are to ensure that expertise and information are shared; that resources are not wasted or efforts duplicated; and that all organizations with a stake in the fight against international crime are able to exploit their comparative advantages most effectively.

INTERPOL has signed cooperation agreements with the United Nations - including related bodies such as UNESCO- the International Criminal Court and regional authorities such as the European Central Bank, Organization of African Unity and Arab Interior Ministers' Council.

COOPERATION AGREEMENTS

Cooperation Agreements with other International Organizations

Interpol has established strong relationships with a wide variety of international organizations, intergovernmental and non governmental, acting in different fields of interest of the Organization.

In order to provide a clear legal basis for working together, Interpol has concluded a number of cooperation agreements with these day-to-day partners.

Agreements with Other International Organizations

Police Cooperation Agreements

The development of a model police cooperation agreement is a concept which has quite naturally gained ground within Interpol. Indeed, it seems obvious that the Organization should provide its member countries with the legal tools they need to facilitate cooperation they initiate bilaterally.

A model agreement has therefore been compiled on the basis of numerous studies, which reflects a wealth of experience in international police cooperation.

In adopting this instrument, in particular for those member states which have not yet developed this form of cooperation to a large extent, the Organization is fulfilling its role as set out in the Constitution, namely 'to ensure and promote the widest possible mutual assistance between all criminal police authorities, and to establish and develop all institutions likely to contribute effectively to the prevention and suppression of ordinary law crimes'.

- List of Police cooperation agreements mentionning Interpol
- Model bilateral police cooperation agreement

Model [bilateral] Police Cooperation Agreement

Wishing to make good use of their membership of the International Criminal Police Organization - INTERPOL, thereby strengthening the services provided by that Organization,

Aware of the need for police cooperation to respect human rights,

Deeming it useful to be able to share their expertise and experience in police matters,

Have agreed as follows:

Note: These provisions are suggested as guidelines and may be changed substantially according to the wishes of the Parties concerned. It does, however, seem important for the preamble to mention that the Agreement is part of the system of cooperation set up by INTERPOL, and that the Parties are INTERPOL Member States.

Furthermore, the reference to human rights explains the provisions concerning the protection of the information exchanged. This reference is necessary in any case in the light of Articles 2 and 3 of INTERPOL's Constitution.

Definitions: For the purposes of this Agreement, "right of observation" shall mean the possibility available to police officers of one Party to observe, in the territory of the other Party and in accordance with the conditions defined in Article 10 of the present Agreement, the movements of an individual who is the subject of a police investigation.

For the purposes of this Agreement, "right of pursuit" shall mean the possibility available to police officers of one Party to pursue an individual with a view to his apprehension in the territory of the other Party, under the conditions defined in Article 11 of the present Agreement.

Note: The model gives two definitions. Although this section is not strictly necessary, it means that both Parties can be sure they are interpreting certain terms in the same way. Further definitions can be included if required.

GENERAL PROVISIONS

Article 1

The Parties hereby establish an Agreement on police cooperation.

Note: This Article situates the Agreement. It is a police agreement and the decision not to mention "criminal police" or "judicial police" was based on the fact that police cooperation goes beyond those limits. Indeed, Parties may find themselves co-operating on forensic science matters, particularly in the area of disaster victim identification, for example.

Article 2

1. The present Agreement comes within the framework of the cooperation system set up by the ICPO-INTERPOL, and the Parties are INTERPOL Member States.

2. The aims of the Agreement are to:
   a. Create a privileged police cooperation space between the Parties;
   b. Set up machinery to facilitate cooperation and to create specific operational structures for that purpose.

Note: Article 2 expressly situates the Agreement within the INTERPOL cooperation system and this is the special characteristic of an agreement based on this model. The Agreement is part of the dynamic nature of the Organization and as such contributes to its development. The reference to INTERPOL's cooperation system provides added value for member countries of the Organization which can benefit from its structure and resources, even in their bilateral relations (provided these relations respect the terms of INTERPOL's Constitution).

Article 3

1. Without prejudice to Article 5 below, the INTERPOL National Central Bureaus (hereinafter referred to as the NCBs) shall act as a liaison channel between the various law enforcement services of the Parties.
2. The NCBs' telecommunications equipment shall be used for cooperation under the terms of the present Agreement.
3. In order to facilitate the cooperation covered by the present Agreement, each Party may, if necessary, request the assistance of the Sub-Regional Bureau for [specify].
4. The law enforcement services referred to in paragraph (1) shall be:
   a. as regards [Party A]: [list of services]

b. as regards [Party B]: [list of services]

Note: The reference to the NCBs is natural in the light of Article 2.

NCBs must be the main channel for cooperation and for the implementation of the bilateral agreement. Hence the sentence stating that their telecommunications equipment shall be used, which means that the INTERPOL network can also be used for bilateral relations. Should the NCBs be unable to fulfil this role effectively, the Parties would have to decide on how to improve the NCBs or how to keep them informed of the activities of the services designated to act as co-ordinators in their place.

The reference to a Sub-Regional Bureau (SRB) is optional: for cooperation to be effective, both Parties should be attached to the same SRB (where there is one) or the Parties may choose not to involve the SRB.

If they wish, the Parties may specify which services are authorized to act under the terms of the cooperation agreement (paragraph (4)). This paragraph enables the Parties to provide for cooperation to involve services such as the customs authorities or the judicial authorities directly. This encourages multidisciplinary cooperation in police matters, where the Parties' legal systems allow this.

EXCHANGE OF INFORMATION

Article 4

1. The Parties undertake to ensure that, when requested, their police authorities shall, in compliance with national legislation and within the limits of their responsibilities, communicate to each other information for preventing ordinary law crime, locating offenders and bringing them to justice. This Article shall not apply where the national legislation

of the requested Party stipulates that the request has to be made to the judicial authorities.

2. Paragraph (1) shall not prevent the Parties, in compliance with their national legislation, from communicating to each other, on their own initiative, potentially useful information, particularly in the interests of maintaining law and order or protecting victims.

Note: This Article details the framework for the exchange of information which is restricted by each Party's national legislation and by the competence of their judicial authorities.

The Article has been drafted in general terms and can be adapted if cooperation is to be restricted as far as the exchange of information is concerned (for example, limited to law enforcement services and/or to the categories of offences covered by the Agreement). The general principle is that, subject to the note under Article 3, NCBs must be as directly involved as possible in the exchange of information.

This Article also provides for some information to be communicated automatically, in particular with a view to preventing any threat to law and order or to protecting the interests of victims. The fact that offences are referred to as "ordinary law crime" is essential because it is a direct reference to the scope of INTERPOL's action as laid down in Article 2(b) and Article 3 of the Organization's Constitution.

Article 5

1. Requests for information and replies to such requests shall be communicated through the Parties' NCBs.
2. Where the request cannot be made in good time by the above procedure or where circumstances so demand, it may be addressed by the competent service

of the requesting Party directly to the competent service of the requested Party, which may reply directly. In such cases, the requesting authority shall as soon as possible inform its country's NCB of its direct application.

3. Requests for information and replies to such requests transmitted in application of paragraph (2) above shall be communicated to the NCB of each Party.

Note: This Article is flexible enough to provide for the use of a more direct channel than through the NCBs. It can sometimes be useful (and quicker) for the relevant law enforcement services (i.e. those responsible for a case) to communicate with each other directly, without using the NCBs as intermediaries.

However, in the interests of centralizing information and keeping all parties informed, the NCBs must be notified when this procedure is used, which often happens when the right of observation/pursuit is exercised (see below). It is indeed essential to centralize information.

The purpose of centralizing information exchanged under the Agreement is to make it available to services or States not directly involved in a particular exchange.

These services or States can then use this information for other investigations which may turn out to be linked to those at the basis of the initial exchange.

Centralizing information is the only way to establish and identify such links.

To be truly effective, bilateral or regional cooperation must be part of a worldwide cooperation system. This is why police cooperation agreements should be part of INTERPOL's cooperation system (see Articles 2 and 3 above), which enables all information exchanged to be centralized and used to maximum effect.

Article 6

The requesting Party (the NCB or some other competent law enforcement service) shall guarantee the level of confidentiality attributed to information by the requested Party (the NCB or other competent law enforcement service).

Note: This provision must be read alongside the following chapter which deals with data protection. This Article concerns all data, whether it is personal or not.

It should however be borne in mind that non-nominal information should be exchanged as freely as possible and that the level of confidentiality of such information should be low enough to encourage wide, multidisciplinary cooperation. Services which are not strictly "police" services (customs, judiciary, etc.) should have access to such information.

It is up to the Parties to determine the measures to be used (technical means, professional secrecy, etc.) to ensure confidentiality.

PROTECTION OF PERSONAL DATA

Article 7

1. In application of the present Agreement, the transmission and processing of personal data shall be subject to the national legislation of each Party and to the relevant rules in force within INTERPOL.
2. Without prejudice to paragraph (1) above, the following rules shall apply to the processing of personal data transmitted in application of the present Agreement:
   a. The data may be used by the recipient Party solely for the purposes for which the present Agreement stipulates that such data may be

transmitted; such data may be used for other purposes only with the prior authorization of the Party which transmitted the data and in compliance with the legislation of the recipient Party.

b. Data may only be used by judicial or police authorities or any other law enforcement authority designated by the Party concerned, a list of which shall be communicated to the other Party.

c. The Party transmitting the data shall be obliged to ensure the accuracy thereof; should it note that the data is inaccurate or should not have been transmitted, the recipient Party must be informed thereof forthwith; the latter shall then be obliged to correct or destroy the data concerned.

d. A Party may not plead that another Party had transmitted inaccurate data in order to avoid its liability under its national legislation vis-à-vis an injured party.

e. The transmission and receipt of personal data shall be recorded. Parties shall communicate to each other a list of authorities or services authorized to consult such records.

f. Communication of and access to data shall be governed by the national legislation of the Party which has been asked for such communication or access by the person concerned. However, data may only be communicated to that person with the authorization of the Party which originally supplied the data.

3. Each Party shall monitor the use made of information communicated by the other Party in order to prevent and sanction any abuse which could infringe on

individual rights. For this purpose, Parties may designate a specific independent supervisory authority.

4. The assessment body set up by virtue of Article 19 below shall be competent to deal with any problems arising from the application or interpretation of the provisions of the present Article. If necessary, this body shall consult with the bodies created by the Parties in application of paragraph (3) above.

Note: Report No. 19, adopted by the General Assembly at its 44th session in Buenos Aires in 1975, did not include any provisions on the protection of personal data. What was not considered essential at the time - particularly in the light of the standard of technology - has now become vital, and a police cooperation agreement which does not set out standards in this area is inconceivable.

This is particularly important since the model agreement is an integral part of INTERPOL's cooperation system. Hence references to Parties' national standards and to the rules of the Organization.

While due consideration is given to States' sovereignty in this Article, it basically reproduces INTERPOL's main data protection rules (which are similar to those used by other international bodies such as the Council of Europe and the United Nations).

This is a way of ensuring that data is accurate, that it is used for the correct purpose, and that the Party which supplied the information retains control over how it is used, so that information exchanged and processed in conformity with this Article can be legitimately accepted and used in judicial proceedings.

The text makes explicit reference to "the relevant rules in force within INTERPOL". Countries may follow the example of Hungary, which has included in its national legislation a provision to the effect that the police shall exchange information with INTERPOL's Member States and General Secretariat according to the rules of that Organization's Constitution and its operating principles, pointing out that membership of INTERPOL constitutes an international undertaking of obligation (see Act LIV of 1999 on Cooperation and Information Exchange with the Law Enforcement Network of the European Union and the International Criminal Police Organization).

Paragraph (2,d) establishes the principle that it is the Party using the data which is responsible. To avoid any legal loopholes in such an agreement, this provision establishes a responsibility towards injured parties.

Even if a Party assumes responsibility towards an injured party, it can always take action against the other Party if the wrong was due to the latter communicating inaccurate information.

Paragraph (2,e) provides for a sort of logbook of operations (transmission and receipt of information) which records the sender, the recipient and any individuals who have accessed the system. Lastly, paragraphs (3) and (4) provide for the introduction of control mechanisms to ensure that cooperation is correctly implemented and to prevent misuse of information.

RIGHT OF OBSERVATION AND PURSUIT

Article 8

1. Police officers of one of the Parties who, within the framework of a criminal investigation, are keeping under observation in their country a person who is presumed to have taken part in a criminal offence referred to in paragraph (8) below, shall be authorized

to pursue their observation in the territory of the other Party where the latter has authorized cross-border observation in response to a request for assistance which has previously been submitted. The request for assistance and the authorization shall be forwarded through the NCB or directly by the authority referred to in paragraph (7) below. Under some circumstances, conditions may be attached to the authorization.

2. On request, the observation will be entrusted to officers of the Party in whose territory it is carried out.

3. Where, for urgent reasons, prior authorization of the other Party cannot be requested, the officers conducting the observation shall be authorized to continue beyond the border the observation of a person as referred to in paragraph (1) above. Exercising the right of observation is subject to the following general conditions:

   a. The NCB of the Party in whose territory the observation is to be continued must be notified immediately, during the observation, that the border has been crossed.

   b. A request for judicial assistance submitted in accordance with paragraph (1) above and outlining the grounds for crossing the border without prior authorization shall be submitted without delay.

   c. When a Party notifies the NCB that the border has been crossed, it should mention whether the officers conducting the observation are carrying their service weapons.

4. Observation shall cease as soon as the Party in whose territory it is taking place so requests, following the

notification referred to in (3,a) or the request referred to in (3,b) or where authorization has not been obtained [twelve] hours after the border was crossed.

5. The observation referred to in this Article shall be carried out only under the following general conditions:

   a. The officers conducting the observation must comply with the provisions of this Article and with the law of the Party in whose territory they are operating; they must obey the instructions of the local responsible authorities.

   b. Except in the situations provided for in paragraph (3) above, the officers shall, during the observation, carry a document certifying that authorization has been granted.

   c. The officers conducting the observation must be able at all times to provide proof that they are acting in an official capacity.

   d. The officers conducting the observation may carry their service weapons during the observation save where specifically otherwise decided by the requested Party; their use shall be prohibited save in cases of legitimate self-defence.

   e. Entry into private homes and places not accessible to the public shall be prohibited.

   f. The officers conducting the observation may neither challenge nor arrest the person under observation.

   g. All observation operations shall be the subject of a report to the authorities of the Party in whose territory they took place; the officers conducting the observation may be required to appear in person.

6. The officers referred to in paragraphs (1), (2), (3) and (5) above shall be:

   a. as regards [Party A]: [list of authorized officers]

   b. as regards [Party B]: [list of authorized officers]

7. The authority empowered to authorize observation in application of paragraph (1) above shall be:

   a. as regards [Party A]: [authority responsible for authorizing observation]

   b. as regards [Party B]: [authority responsible for authorizing observation]

Option 1

8. Observation as referred to above may take place only in connection with offences likely to result in extradition proceedings between the Parties.

Option 2

9. Observation as referred to above may take place only in connection with the following offences:

Note: Observation operations enable police officers to gather important information for their investigations. It therefore seems essential that such an agreement should provide for this form of cooperation.

However, it is a procedure which affects sovereignty and needs to be extremely well organized, hence the length of this Article and the detailed provisions. The above conditions may be adapted according to what the Parties are prepared to agree on.

For example, although observation should obviously only be considered for relatively serious offences, such as those which might result in extradition (see paragraph (1)), it is not necessarily essential to list those offences which would result in the implementation of this procedure (see paragraph (8)). There are two options available: either Parties consider that observation may be carried out for extraditable offences (option 1), or Parties draw up a list of offences (option 2). Such a list is usually less extensive, and could give rise to difficulties since, in practice, it is impossible to cover all possibilities.

Similarly, Parties are free to determine the geographical area in which observation is authorized, i.e. just the border area or the whole country.

Given the effects of this Article, prerequisites or special procedures will have to be laid down for its acceptance and implementation.

The possibilities offered by this Article imply that the Parties are already linked by an international agreement empowering their police authorities to take responsibility for this procedure. If the Parties are not linked by such an agreement, they will probably have to ask their Ministries of Foreign Affairs if this procedure is acceptable as far as legislation and other international commitments are concerned.

Article 9

1. Officers of one of the Parties following, in their country, an individual caught in the act of committing one of the offences referred to in paragraph (7) below, or participating in one of those offences, shall be authorized to continue pursuit in the territory of the other Party without prior authorization where, given the urgency of the situation, it was not possible to notify the competent authorities of the other Party or where these authorities have been unable to reach the scene in time to take over the pursuit.
2. The same shall apply where the person pursued has

escaped from provisional custody or while serving a custodial sentence.

3. The pursuing officers shall, not later than when they cross the border, notify the competent authorities of the Party in whose territory the pursuit is to take place. The pursuit will cease as soon as the Party in whose territory the pursuit is taking place so requests. At the request of the pursuing officers, the competent local authorities shall apprehend the pursued person so that he can be arrested.

4. NCBs shall be informed, not later than when the border is crossed, of the cross-border pursuit and shall in turn notify:

   a. as regards [Party A]: [competent authority],

   b. as regards [Party B]: [competent authority].

5. The officers pursuing an individual in conformity with the terms of this Article shall not have the right to apprehend that person.

6. Pursuit may be carried out for as long as it takes to achieve the desired result and without limit in space (subject to the restriction provided for in paragraph (8,c) of the present Article).

Option 1

7. Pursuit as referred to above may take place only in connection with offences likely to result in extradition proceedings between the Parties.

Option 2

7. Pursuit as referred to above may take place only in connection with the following offences:

8. Pursuit as referred to in the present Article shall be subject to the following general conditions:

a. The pursuing officers must comply with the provisions of this Article and with the law of the Party in whose territory they are operating; they must obey the instructions of the local responsible authorities.

b. Pursuit shall be solely over land borders, including lakes and waterways.

c. Entry into private homes and places not accessible to the public shall be prohibited.

d. The pursuing officers shall be easily identifiable, either by their uniform or by means of an armband or by accessories fitted to their vehicle; the use of civilian clothes combined with the use of unmarked vehicles without the aforementioned identification is prohibited; the pursuing officers must at all times be able to prove that they are acting in an official capacity.

e. The pursuing officers may carry their service weapons; their use shall be prohibited save in cases of legitimate self-defence.

f. After a pursuit, the pursuing officers shall present themselves before the local competent authorities of the Party in whose territory they were operating and shall give an account of their mission; at the request of those authorities, they must remain at their disposal until the circumstances of their action have been adequately elucidated; this condition shall apply even where the pursuit has not resulted in the arrest of the pursued person.

g. The authorities of the Party from which the pursuing officers have come shall, at the request of the authorities of the Party in whose territory the pursuit took place, assist the enquiry subsequent to the operation in which they took part, including legal proceedings.

9. The officers referred to in the previous paragraphs shall be:

   a. as regards [Party A]: [list of authorized officers]

   b. as regards [Party B]: [list of authorized officers]

Note: The structure of this Article is similar to that of the Article on observation (Article 8). It should however be pointed out that the conditions attached to the right of pursuit are more restrictive because pursuit encroaches on national sovereignty to an even greater extent than observation. Generally speaking, the same comments apply, particularly those relating to the implementation or acceptance of the procedure by the Parties' competent authorities (see note after Article 8). Paragraph (6) may be adapted according to any restrictions in space and time which the Parties may wish to attach to the right of pursuit.

Article 10

1. During cross-border observation or pursuit, officers shall be subject to the same legal provisions in terms of traffic regulations as the officers of the Party in whose territory the observation or pursuit is being carried out. The Parties shall inform each other (through their NCBs) of the legislation in force in this area.

2. Technical resources to facilitate cross-border observation or pursuit may be used, provided that this is authorized by the legislation of the Party in whose territory the observation or pursuit is being carried out.

3. The Parties undertake to establish conditions for law enforcement services to use aircraft for observation,

pursuit or other cross-border operations decided on in conjunction with the relevant services.

Note: This Article reproduces the general provisions common to the two techniques covered by the previous two Articles. The technical resources referred to in paragraph (2) cover means of communication as well as means of observation, such as binoculars, cameras, etc.

The Article also paves the way for the use of aircraft for cross-border operations.

This practice is not yet common enough for principles to have been established about it. Furthermore, these provisions are similar to those in Articles 8 and 9 above, in that the Parties should be linked by an agreement in order to implement them.

Article 11

During the operations referred to in Articles 8 and 9 above, the agents on mission in the territory of the other Party shall be subject to the law on civil liability and criminal responsibility of the Party in whose territory they are operating.

Note: This Article introduces the principle of responsibility which is developed in the following Article. This provision is essential given the nature of the procedures Parties are authorizing each other to carry out (observation and pursuit).

It is necessary to define principles of responsibility to encourage the continued implementation of the Agreement in the event of problems involving responsibility. Without such a provision, subsequent disagreements might result in Parties denouncing the cooperation agreement. In the light of the legal implications of this provision, Parties are strongly advised to consult their Ministries of Foreign Affairs on the matter.

Article 12

1. Where, in accordance with Articles 8 and 9 above, officers of one Party are operating in the territory of the other Party, the first Party shall be responsible for any damage caused by them during the course of their mission, in accordance with the law of the Party in whose territory they are operating.

2. The Party in whose territory the damage referred to in paragraph (1) above occurs shall repair such damage under the conditions applicable to damage caused by its own officers.

3. The Party whose officers have caused damage to anyone in the territory of the other Party shall reimburse in full to the latter any sums the latter has paid out to the victims or other entitled persons.

4. Without prejudice to the exercise of its rights vis-à-vis third parties and without prejudice to paragraph (3) above, each Party shall refrain, in the case provided for in paragraph (1) above, from requesting reimbursement of the amount of damages it has sustained from the other Party.

Note: This Article details the practical implementation of the principle of responsibility defined in the previous Article. It deals mainly with the issue of reparation by defining the responsibilities of each Party so that no individual is in any way wronged as a result of the Agreement being applied (see paragraph (2)).

Paragraph (4) deals with damages caused directly to the other Party and not to a private individual who is a national of that Party. This includes damage to movable or immovable property belonging to public officials, as well as damage caused to officers of the State concerned. In the light of the legal implications of this provision, Parties are strongly advised to consult their Ministries of Foreign Affairs on the matter.

MISSIONS, PARTICIPATION IN INVESTIGATIONS, SPECIAL INVESTIGATIVE TECHNIQUES

Article 13

1. Officers from one Party may enter the territory of the other Party in order to assist in investigations being carried out in that territory.
2. When officers are on mission in application of the present Article, they shall act as observers.
3. Officers on mission shall be authorized to be present during:
    a. searches of premises,
    b. searches of persons,
    c. questioning and hearings,
    d. autopsies.
4. Officers on mission may be authorized to ask questions during questioning and hearings. However, only officers from the territory in which the procedure is taking place shall be authorized to decide what action to take.
5. Missions shall be organized by the Parties' NCBs.

Note: This Article provides for a system whereby officers from one Party may be passively involved in investigations being carried out by the other Party. Paragraph (5) reiterates one of the NCBs' traditional roles, i.e. coordinating international cooperation. To this effect, they are able to make the arrangements involved in implementing this Article. In their capacity as central liaison points, they are familiar with the possibilities and the rules to be respected and should be the only contacts used in this context. Paragraph (5) deals with an issue which has been discussed at length within the Organization.

Two General Assembly resolutions acknowledge the importance of NCBs being responsible for organizing police missions abroad (Resolution AGN/42/RES/8 of 1973 and Resolution AGN/49/RES/4 of 1980). In addition, in the early 1980s, the General Secretariat carried out a study of the question which was then the subject of a 1981 General Assembly report (Report No. 16).

This study showed that NCBs were generally in the best position to organize police missions abroad. In this way they fulfil their role as central contact points for international police cooperation.

Article 14

1. Parties shall take the necessary measures to coordinate the implementation of special investigative techniques, such as controlled deliveries, surveillance and undercover operations, for the purpose of gathering evidence so that the competent authorities may take legal action against persons involved in an offence targeted by these techniques.
2. Officers of one Party involved in this type of investigation shall respect the conditions agreed on with the Party in whose territory that investigation is taking place.
3. Parties shall agree on the extent to which the implementation of the provisions of the present Article may give rise to financial compensation or a sharing of the costs involved.

Note: INTERPOL became interested in controlled deliveries back in 1979 when the subject was an item on the agenda of the Meeting of Heads of European National Drug Services. As a result of this meeting, a questionnaire was produced and the replies became the subject of Report No. 9, which was submitted to the 48th General Assembly session held in Nairobi in 1979.

The notion of "controlled deliveries" was first codified in international law with the 1988 United Nations Convention against Illicit Traffic in Narcotic Drugs and Psychotropic Substances. With the draft United Nations Convention against Transnational Organized Crime, currently under negotiation, the idea has been reinforced and expanded to become "special investigative techniques".

This is an important concept which has a considerable impact on operational activities.

The General Secretariat asked European States (outside the European Union) about their legislation and practices regarding controlled deliveries and the use of undercover agents.

These studies showed that these investigative techniques are an important part of States' legal weaponry for combating complex crimes. Studies have also been carried out at a worldwide level because all INTERPOL member countries are beginning to experience the need for such techniques.

Article 14 satisfies this need, even though its implementation would require specific national legislation in most States. Including such a provision in a police cooperation agreement encourages States to legislate in this area, which will in turn open up increased opportunities for effective cooperation.

Paragraph (3) is necessary insofar as the Party in whose territory a controlled delivery is taking place, for example, will be using a certain amount of logistical resources and incurring costs without directly benefiting from the results of the operation. This being the case, Parties may consider it appropriate to agree to the requesting Party giving the other Party financial compensation for the assistance provided, notably by sharing the proceeds of confiscated assets when they are sold off for the benefit of the public sector.

Article 15

1. The Parties shall consult each other on the creation of mixed teams to implement the provisions of the present Chapter.
2. Officers of the Parties who are members of such teams shall comply with the instructions of the competent authorities of the Party in whose territory the operation is taking place.

Note: This Article goes a stage further than the two previous ones by providing for the creation of mixed, institutionalized teams made up of officers from each Party. These teams are not formed for the purposes of a particular case but instead are permanent teams whose members co-operate on a daily basis. The main purpose of these mixed teams is to ensure the effectiveness of the operations referred to in Article 14.

Paragraph (2) establishes who will be in charge of the teams, which will depend on the territory in which they are operating.

OTHER FORMS OF COOPERATION

Article 16

1. The Parties shall co-operate in forensic science and other technical matters. In this respect, each Party shall make available to the other Party its material and human resources for carrying out investigations in this area.

2. To this effect, when necessary the Parties shall provide each other with evidence, or the quantities of substances required for analysis or investigation.
3. The Parties shall also co-operate in the identification of victims of major disasters.
4. The Parties shall agree on whether the use of such resources provided by one Party to another shall give rise to financial compensation.

Note: The advantage of cooperation in forensic science and other technical matters is that expensive equipment can be shared and would therefore be more economically viable.

For this to happen, reports produced by the relevant services of one Party need to be accepted by the judicial authorities of the other Party.

Apart from requests for mutual assistance in this area, the Parties may find it useful to send each other samples of substances seized (such as drugs), as provided for in paragraph (2).

Such samples can provide the recipient Party with a considerable amount of information and may enable links to be established with other cases.

Paragraph (3) deals with cooperation which is not linked to judicial enquiries, i.e. the use of forensic science in civil cases. This provision explains why Article 1 of the model agreement does not refer to "criminal" or "judicial" police.

Paragraph (4) raises the issue of financial compensation as a result of the implementation of this Article. If work done in application of this Article results in the requesting Party being billed for it, the price charged should be as low as possible (cost price) so that no Party may make an unjustified profit from the cooperation carried out in the context of this Agreement.

Article 17

1. The Parties shall organize reciprocal visits between their respective border units.

2. A Party may invite officers selected by the other Party to attend its seminars and in-house training courses in subject areas such as:

   o Methods used to prevent, detect and combat offences,

   o Routes and modus operandi used by individuals suspected of committing offences,

   o Control of import/export of contraband,

   o Gathering evidence,

   o Law enforcement equipment and techniques (electronic surveillance, controlled deliveries, undercover operations, etc.). (non-exhaustive list)

3. The Parties shall consider associating all those involved in law enforcement, including judges and customs officers, in the above-mentioned visits and training.

4. A Party shall send officers as interns to the other Party in order to familiarize them with the latter's structure and practices.

Note: It is important for Parties' officials to be familiar with their counterparts and their working methods in the interests of encouraging the daily implementation of the police cooperation referred to in the model agreement.

Similarly, the Parties may consider it useful to share experience and organize joint training courses as an even greater encouragement to their officers to work as a team. Such training courses also offer an opportunity to share expertise where one Party has more experience in a particular area than the other. Involving other law enforcement services encourages and improves multidisciplinary cooperation, which inevitably increases the effectiveness of international cooperation, especially in connection with particularly complex offences.

Article 18

The Parties shall encourage appropriate language training for officers likely to be in contact with officers from the other Party (particularly NCB officers).

Note: The language issue is of fundamental importance because it is often an obstacle to good cooperation between the officers responsible for such contact. It is vital that communication be as effective as possible, for state-of-the-art telecommunications equipment is of little use if the people using it cannot understand each other.

IMPLEMENTATION ASSESSMENT AND RESOLVING IMPLEMENTATION PROBLEMS

Article 19

Option 1

1. A common body shall be responsible for assessing the cooperation implemented under the present Agreement on a yearly basis.
2. The common assessment body shall communicate its findings to the competent government authorities of each Party, who shall take any necessary measures to resolve problems arising from the implementation of the present Agreement.
3. [Name and composition of this common body]

Option 2

1. A common body shall be responsible for assessing the

cooperation implemented under the present Agreement on a yearly basis.

2. The common assessment body shall be composed of representatives of the Ministers responsible for the implementation of the present Agreement, Heads of NCBs and heads of the services referred to in Article 3(1) above.

Note: It would appear essential to assess cooperation so that it can be adapted in the event of problems and/or shortcomings. Setting up a common assessment body to this effect will establish a dialogue between the Parties. The assessment body can be set up at ministerial level (Option 2) or can operate at a more technical level while reporting to the ministerial (i.e. political) level likely to be able to resolve any problems (Option 1).

Whichever option is chosen, the importance of the role of the NCBs (see Article 3) means that the Heads of NCBs should be actively involved in the work of the assessment body.

Article 20

1. Difficulties arising from the application or interpretation of the present Agreement shall be the subject of consultation between the authorities of the Pa ties in the context of the common body created by virtue of Article 19 above.

2. Each Party may request that a meeting of experts be held to resolve problems related to the application of the present Agreement and to submit to the common body proposals for developing cooperation.

Note: Paragraph (1) assigns a supplementary role to the common assessment body which, understandably enough, also provides a forum for discussion of any difficulties encountered in implementing the Agreement. This role should be given to the same body because a different one would not necessarily be familiar with how the Agreement works or be able to assess any problems in a satisfactory manner. However, the common assessment body may consider it necessary to set up an ad hoc body to shed new light on problems, and this is provided for in paragraph (2).

The structure of any such ad hoc body should be flexible so that it can be adapted according to the circumstances and decided on as and when necessary. For example, it could be composed of officers working on a day-to-day, operational basis, or university professors to help with legal questions, etc.

FINAL PROVISIONS

Article 21

The present Agreement shall not affect the application of agreements already in force between the Parties.

Note: This provision is meant to take account of any possible overlapping when there is more than one agreement on the same subject. It establishes the principle that such agreements are independent of each other. This is a conventional provision but Parties may provide for the new Agreement to replace an existing agreement. In that case, the following wording is suggested for Article 21: "As from its entry into force, the present Agreement shall replace the [title of agreement] agreement concluded between the Parties on [date]".

Article 22

1. The present Agreement shall enter into force on the date of notification of the second instrument of ratification.

2. The present Agreement has no expiry date.

3. Denunciation shall be notified in writing to the other Party or at least six months before it is to take effect. Denunciation shall in no way detract from the Parties' rights and obligations resulting from cooperation carried on under the terms of the present Agreement.

Note: This Article contains standard provisions. Paragraph (1), for example, authorizes the implementation of the Agreement between two Parties even if the other Parties (in the case of a multilateral agreement) have not yet ratified it. This will prevent one Party blocking the Agreement when four or five States are involved.

At paragraph (2), the Parties may decide to give the Agreement a fixed term. In this case, provision also needs to be made for negotiations to renew the Agreement to begin, say, a year before it expires. The Parties also need to provide for what will happen to the Agreement if negotiations are inconclusive at the date of expiry. The Agreement could be allowed to expire, be renewed automatically for its initial duration or, ideally, extended for six to twelve months so that negotiations can be completed. If negotiations then fail, the Agreement would be rendered null and void.

Paragraph (3) reconciles the provisions of Article 12 on the Parties' liability with denunciation of the Agreement. A Party will not be able to free itself of its responsibility by denouncing the Agreement, since its obligations defined under Article 12 will survive the Agreement. Similarly, if a Party still has information from the other Party when the denunciation takes effect, the relevant provisions of Article 7 still apply.

7

INTERNATIONAL CONVENTIONS AND INTERPOL's TRANSMISSION ROLE

CONVENTIONS ADOPTED UNDER THE AUSPICES OF THE COUNCIL OF EUROPE

European Convention on Extradition (Paris, 1957) (European Treaties, ETS No. 24)

Article 16 (3)

A request for provisional arrest shall be sent to the competent authorities of the requested Party either through the diplomatic channel or direct by post or telegraph or through the International Criminal Police Organization (INTERPOL) or by any other means affording evidence in writing or accepted by the requested Party. The requesting authority shall be informed without delay of the result of its request.

European Convention on Mutual Assistance in Criminal Matters (Strasbourg, 1959) (European Treaties, ETS No. 30)

Article 15 (5)

In cases where direct transmission is permitted under this convention, it may take place through the International Criminal Police Organization (INTERPOL).

European Convention on the Supervision of Conditionally Sentenced or Condi-tionally Released Offenders (Strasbourg, 1964) (European Treaties, ETS No. 51)

Article 27 (3)

In case of emergency, the communications referred to in paragraph 2 of this Article may be made through the International Criminal Police Organization (INTERPOL).

European Convention on the Punishment of Road Traffic Offences (Strasbourg, 1964) (European Treaties, ETS No. 52)

Article 15 (3)

In case of emergency, the communications referred to in paragraph 2 of this Article may be made through the International Criminal Police Organization (INTERPOL).

European Convention on the International Validity of Criminal Judgements (The Hague, 1970) (European Treaties, ETS No. 70)

Article 15 (2)

In urgent cases, requests and communications may be sent through the International Criminal Police Organization (INTERPOL).

European Convention on the Repatriation of Minors (The Hague, 1970) (European Treaties, ETS No. 71)

Article 21

Communications between central authorities, in connection with the implementation of this Convention may be transmitted through the International Criminal Police Organization (INTERPOL).

European Convention on the Transfer of Proceedings in Criminal Matters (Strasbourg, 1972) (European Treaties, ETS No. 73)

Article 13 (2)

In urgent cases, requests and communications may be sent through the International Criminal Police Organization (INTERPOL).

European Convention on the Control of the Acquisition and Possession of Firearms by Individuals (Strasbourg, 1978) (European Treaties, ETS No. 101)

Article 9 (2)

When appropriate the notifications may be sent through the International Criminal Police Organization (INTERPOL).

Convention on Laundering, Search, Seizure and Confiscation of the Proceeds from Crime (Strasbourg, 1990) (European Treaties, ETS No. 141)

Article 24 (3)

Any request or communication under Paragraphs 1 and 2 of this Article may be made through the International Criminal Police Organisation (INTERPOL).

Agreement on Illicit Traffic by Sea, implementing Article 17 of the United Nations Convention against Illicit Traffic in Narcotic Drugs and Psychotropic Substances (Strasbourg, 1995) (European Treaties, ETS No. 156)

Article 18

(Communication between Designated Authorities):

The authorities designated under Article 17 shall communicate directly with one another.

Where, for any reason, direct communication is not practicable, Parties may agree to use the communication channels of ICPO-INTERPOL or of the Customs Cooperation Council [World Customs Organization].

Criminal Law Convention on Corruption (Strasbourg, 1999) (European Treaties, ETS No. 173)

Article 30 (3)

(Direct communication):

Any request or communication under Paragraphs 1 and 2 of this article may be made through the International Criminal Police Organisation (INTERPOL).

Draft Convention on Cyber-crime (PC-CY(99)28)

Article ... (2)

(Direct Communications):

Any request or communication under Paragraph 1 of this article may be made through the International Criminal Police Organisation (INTERPOL).

2. Convention adopted under the auspices of the United Nations

United Nations Convention Against Illicit Traffic in Narcotic Drugs and Psychotropic Substances (Vienna, 1988) (Registration No. 27627)

Article 7 (8)

[...] Transmission of requests for mutual legal assistance and any communication related thereto shall be effected between the authorities designated by the Parties; this requirement shall be without prejudice to the right of a Party to require that such requests and communications be addressed to it through the diplomatic channel and, in urgent circumstances, where the Parties agree, through channels of the International Criminal Police Organization, if possible.

United Nations model treaty on extradition (1990)

Article 9 (1)

(Provisional arrest):

In case of urgency the requesting State may apply for the provisional arrest of the person sought pending the presentation of the request for extradition. The application shall be transmitted by means of the facilities of the International Criminal Police Organization, by post or telegraph or by any other means affording a record in writing.

Rules of procedure and evidence (adopted in 1994) of the International Tribunal for the Prosecution for Persons Responsible for Serious Violations of International Humanitarian Law committed in the territory of Former Yugoslavia since 1991 (Tribunal established by UN Security Council resolution 827)

Rule 39

In the conduct of an investigation, the Prosecutor may [...] seek the assistance of any relevant international body including the International Criminal Police Organization (INTERPOL).

Rome Statute on the International Criminal Court (Rome, 1998) (A/CONF.183/9)

Article 87 (b)(1)

(Cooperation Requests: General Provisions/Assigned Authorities for Presenting or Receiving Requests/ Transmission of Requests): when appropriate, without prejudice to the provisions of subparagraph (a), requests may also be transmitted through the International Criminal Police Organization - INTERPOL - or any appropriate regional organization.

Draft International Convention for the Suppression of Terrorist Financing (1999) (A/C.6/54/L.16)

Article 18 (4)

States Parties may exchange information through the International Criminal Police Organization (INTERPOL).

The United Nations Convention against Transnational

Organized Crime (A/55/3823), adopted by the General Assembly in 2000 and entered into force in 2003

Article 18 (13)

Each States Party shall designate a central authority that shall have the responsibility and power to receive requests for mutual legal assistance and either to execute them or to transmit them to the competent authorities for execution. [...] Central authorities shall ensure the speedy and proper execution or transmission of the requests received [...]. Requests for mutual legal assistance and any communication related thereto shall be transmitted to the central authorities designated by the States Parties. This requirement shall be without prejudice to the right of a State Party to require that such requests and communication be addressed to it through diplomatic channels and, in urgent circumstances, where the States Parties agree, through the International Criminal Police Organization, if possible.

Among the three supplementary Protocols, only one - The Revised Draft Protocol against the Illicit Manufacturing of and Trafficking in Firearms, Ammunition and Other related Materials (A/AC.254/4/Add.2/Rev.2) - expressly refers to INTERPOL.

Option 1 (f)

Recognizing the importance of strengthening existing international law enforcement support mechanisms, such as the database established by the International Criminal Police Organization, the INTERPOL Weapons and Explosives Tracking System, [and the database established by the Customs Cooperation Council (known as the World Customs Organization), the Central Information System,] to prevent, combat and eradicate the illicit manufacturing of and trafficking in firearms, ammunition [, explosives] and other related materials.

Article 2 (f)

[...] Convinced that combating the illicit manufacturing of and trafficking in firearms, ammunition and other related materials requires international cooperation and the strengthening of existing international law enforcement support mechanisms such as the database established by the International Criminal Police Organization, the INTERPOL Weapons and Explosives Tracking System, in order to prevent, combat and eradicate the illicit manufacturing of and trafficking in firearms, ammunition and other related materials.

3. Convention adopted under the auspices of the European Union

Belgium - France -Federal Republic of Germany-Luxembourg-Netherlands: Schengen agreement on the gradual abolition of checks at their common borders and the Convention applying the agreement (Agreement: Schengen, 14th June 1985; Convention: Schengen, 19th June 1990).

Article 53(2)

Paragraph 1 shall not prejudice the possibility of requests being sent and returned between Ministries of Justice or through the intermediary of national central offices of the International Criminal Police Organization.

Convention on the setting up of a European Police Office (Europol) (Brussels, 1995) (SN 3549/95)

Article 42(2)

In so far as is required for the performance of the tasks described in Article 3, Europol may also establish and maintain relations with third States and third bodies within the meaning of Article 10(4), points 4, 5, 6 and 7.

(Point 7 expressly refers to the International Criminal Police Organization).

Draft Council Act Establishing the Convention on Mutual Assistance in Criminal Matters between the Member States of the European Union (1999/C 251/01)

Article 6(4)

(Transmission of Requests for Mutual Assistance): Any request as referred to in Paragraph 1 may, for the sake of speed, be made via the International Criminal Police Organization (INTERPOL) or any body competent under provisions introduced pursuant to the Treaty on European Union.

4. Instrument adopted under the auspices of the Commonwealth

Commonwealth Scheme for the Rendition of Fugitive Offenders

Clause 4(1)

(Provisional warrants): Where a fugitive offender is, or is suspected of being, in or on his way to any part of the Commonwealth but no warrant has been endorsed [...] or issued [...], the competent judicial authority in that part of the Commonwealth may issue a provisional warrant for his arrest on such information and under such circumstances as would, in the authority's opinion, justify the issue of a warrant if the returnable offence of which the fugitive is accused has been an offence committed within the authority's jurisdiction and for the purposes of this paragraph information contained in an international notice issued by the International Criminal Police Organisation (INTERPOL) in respect of a fugitive may be considered by the authority, either alone or with other information, in deciding whether a provisional warrant should be issued for the arrest of that fugitive.

5. Convention adopted under the auspices of the Economic Community of West African States Convention on Extradition (Abuja, 1994)

Article 22(3)

The request for provisional arrest shall be transmitted to the competent authorities of the requested State either through the diplomatic channel, or direct by post or telegraph, or through the International Criminal Police Organization (INTERPOL), or by any other means affording evidence in writing or accepted by the requested State [...].

6. Convention adopted under the auspices of the Organization of American States (OAS)

Inter-American Convention against the illicit manufacturing of and trafficking in firearms, ammunition, explosives and other related materials (Washington, 1997) (AG00784.E)

Preamble

Recognizing the importance of strengthening existing international law enforcement support mechanisms such as the International Weapons and Explosives Tracking System (IWETS) of the International Criminal Police Organization (INTERPOL), to prevent, combat, and eradicate the illicit manufacturing of and trafficking in firearms, ammunition, explosives, and other related materials.

7. Example of a multilateral convention mentioning INTERPOL

Cooperation agreement on police matters between Benin, Ghana, Nigeria and Togo (Lagos, 1984)

Article 3

The INTERPOL National Central Bureaus shall serve as a liaison organ between the different security services of the Contracting Parties.

Agreement on Cooperation on Control of Illicit Trafic in Narcotic Drugs and Psychotrophic Substances between the

Ministries of the Interior of the Republics of Azerbaijan, Armenia, Belarus, Georgia, Kazakhstan, Moldova, Russia, Tajikistan, Turkmenistan, Uzbekistan, Ukraine and Estonia (Kiev, 1992)

Article 3(d)

[...] Information shall be submitted on unified carriers recommended by INTERPOL.

Agreement on Cooperation to Prevent and Combat Trans-border Crime between the Governments of Romania, Albania, Bulgaria, Bosnia-Herzegovina, Greece, FYROM, Moldova, Turkey and Hungary (Bucharest, 1999)

Article 2(4)

In order to improve the effectiveness of the prevention, detection, investigation and prosecution of trans-border criminal violations, and as active members of ICPO-INTERPOL for police matters, World Customs Organization for customs matters, the SECI [Southeast European Co-operative Initiative] participating countries shall exchange and develop criminal information in partnership with their law enforcement authorities and with the INTERPOL General Secretariat and WCO.

8. Examples of bilateral conventions in which INTERPOL is mentioned

Treaty between Canada and France concerning Extradition (1988)

Article 13(1)

(Provisional Arrest): In cases of urgency, the competent authorities of the requesting State may request the provisional arrest of the person sought, through diplomatic channels or directly by post or telegraph, or through the International Criminal Police Organization (INTERPOL), or by any other method that provides a written record of the request [....].

Treaty on Extradition between France and Australia (1988)

Article 9(1)(b)

The application for provisional arrest shall be transmitted by means of the facilities of the International Criminal Police Organization (INTERPOL), by post or telegraph or by any other means affording a record in writing

THE UNITED NATIONS

INTERPOL has long co-operated with the United Nations in law enforcement matters, a relationship that was formalized by the signing of a cooperation agreement between the two organizations in October 1996.

The cooperation agreement grants the two organizations observer status in sessions of their respective general assemblies. The agreement outlines further areas in which the two organizations could coordinate their efforts:

- responding to the needs of the international community in fighting crime
- assisting states in their efforts to combat organized crime
- co-operating in the implementation of the mandates of international judicial bodies
- carrying out joint investigations and other police-related matters in the context of peace-keeping
- establishing joint databases related to penal law.

To strengthen the global capacity to respond coherently to ever-changing developments in the world from a law enforcement perspective, INTERPOL appointed Dr Ulrich Kersten, former president of the German Federal Criminal Police (Bundeskriminalamt) and former INTERPOL Executive Committee member, as its first Special Representative to the United Nations on November 5, 2004.

As both organizations occupy unique positions in the international community, the creation of the INTERPOL office at UN headquarters in New York marks the beginning of a new era of cooperation between them.

The INTERPOL office at the UN embodies the spirit of the original cooperation agreement, and will focus on:

- liaison between INTERPOL and the United Nations by establishing, maintaining, developing and promoting contact networks between the general secretariats of the two organizations, their dependent bodies and their officials
- raising UN awareness of INTERPOL's functions and services by facilitating and enhancing the exchange of information between the two parties
- identifying opportunities for collaboration based on extensive knowledge of the activities and developments of the two organizations
- acting as the senior advisor to the INTERPOL Secretary General regarding all matters or developments having, or that may have, a UN impact.

POLICE - JUSTICE

International

- Europol
- International Association of Chiefs of Police (IACP)

- International Association of Law Enforcement Intelligence Analysts (IALEIA)
- International Association of Women Police
- United Nations International Criminal Tribunal for the former Yugoslavia

Argentina

- Gendarmeria Nacional Argentina
- Interpol Argentina (O.C.N. Buenos Aires)
- Ministerio de Justicia
- Policia Federal Argentina

Australia

- Australian Customs Service
- Australian Federal Police
- New South Wales Police Service
- Northern Territory Police Service
- Police Association of New South Wales
- Police Association of South Australia
- Queensland Police Service
- South Australia Police
- Tasmania Police
- Victoria Police
- Western Australia Police Service

Austria

- Bundesministerium für Inneres

Belgium

- Police Fédérale
- SPF (Service Public Fédéral) Intérieur
- Ministère de la Justice

Bolivia

- Corte Suprema de Justicia
- Fiscalía General de la Republica
- Ministerio de Gobierno
- Policía Nacional de Bolivia
- Ministerio de Relaciones Exteriores

Brazil

- Departamento de Polícia Federal

Brunei

- Royal Brunei Police Force

Bulgaria

- Ministry of the Interior

Canada

- Interpol Ottawa (English - Français)
- Canadian Firearms Centre
- Canadian Security Intelligence Service (CSIS)
- Criminal Intelligence Service Canada (CISC)
- Department of Justice (Canada)
- Kingston Police (Ontario)

- Royal Canadian Mounted Police (RCMP)
- Sûreté du Québec

Chile

- Carabineros de Chile
- Policía de Investigaciones de Chile

Colombia

- Departamento Administrativo de Seguridad

Cyprus

- Cyprus Police

Czech Republic

- Ministerstvo vnitra Ceské republiky

Denmark

- Danish National Police

Finland

- Finnish Police

France

- Ministère de la Justice
- Ministère de l'Intérieur
- La Police nationale
- Organisation
- Direction Centrale de la Police Judiciaire (DCPJ)
- Ecole Nationale Supérieure de la Police (ENSP)
- Service de Coopération Technique Internationale de Police (SCTIP)

Germany

- Bundeskriminalamt (BKA)
- Bundesministerium der Justiz

Gibraltar

- Royal Gibraltar Police
- Gibraltar Coordinating Centre for Criminal Intelligence and Drugs (GCID)

Guatemala

- Organismo judicial
- Ministerio Público
- Ministerio Gobernación
- Policía Nacional Civil
- Migración

Hong Kong

- Department of Justice
- Hong Kong Police

Ireland

- An Garda Síochána (Ireland's National Police Services)
- Department of Justice, Equality and Law Reform

Israel

- Ministry of Justice

Italy

- Arma dei Carabinieri
- Ministero dell'Interno

- Ministero della Giustizia
- Polizia di Stato
- Guardia di Finanza

Jamaica

- Jamaica Constabulary Force

Japan

- Ministry of Justice
- National Police Agency

Lebanon

- Internal Security Forces (ISF)
- Ministry of Justice

Luxembourg

- Police Grand-Ducale de Luxembourg

New Zealand

- Ministry of Justice
- New Zealand Police
- Interpol-Wellington New Zealand

Nicaragua

- Corte Suprema de Justicia
- Ministerio de Gobernación
- Policía Nacional de Nicaragua

Norway

- Kriminalpolitisentralen (KRIPOS)

Panamá

- Policía Técnica Judicial
- Ministerio Público
- Órgano Judicial
- Ministerio de Gobierno y Justicia
- Procuraduría de la Administración
- Policía Nacional

Papua New Guinea

- Department of Police

Peru

- Ministerio del Interior de Perú
- Policía Nacional del Perú
- Interpol Lima

Portugal

- Polícia Judiciária

Singapore

- Ministry of Home Affairs
- Central Narcotics Bureau

Slovakia

- Ministry of Interior

Slovenia

- Ministry of the Interior

South Africa

- South Africa Police Service

Spain

- Ministerio del Interior (Espagne)
- Dirección General de la Policía
- Dirección General de la Guardia Civil
- Plan Nacional Sobre Drogas (PNSD)
- Dirección General de Instituciones Penitenciarias
- Dirección General de Administración de la Seguridad

Sweden

- Polisen i Sverige

Switzerland

- Schweizerische Bundespolizei - Polizia federale svizzera - Police fédérale suisse

Thailand

- Royal Thai Police
- Ministry of Interior

Turkey

- Turk Polis Teskilati

United Kingdom

- Centre for Crime and Justice Studies
- HM Customs and Excise
- Home Office
- Serious Organized Crime Agency
- Metropolitan Police
- Police Act 1997
- Police Service of Northern Ireland

United States of America

- Department of Homeland Security (DHS)
- U.S. Citizenship and Immigration Services (USCIS)
- U.S. Customs and Border Protection (CBP)
- Federal Law Enforcement Training Center (FLETC)
- U.S. Immigration and Customs Enforcement (ICE)
- U.S. Secret Service
- Transportation Security Administration (TSA)
- Department of Justice (DoJ)
- Interpol-US National Central Bureau
- Antitrust Division
- Civil Rights Division
- Criminal Division
- Environment and Natural Resources Division
- Tax Division
- Federal Bureau of Investigation (FBI)
- U.S. Marshals Service
- Federal Bureau of Prisons (BOP)
- Drug Enforcement Administration (DEA)
- U.S. Citizenship and Immigration Services
- Executive Office for U.S. Attorneys (EOUSA)
- Executive Office for U.S. Trustees
- Office of Tribal Justice (OTJ)
- Office of Information and Privacy (OIP)
- Office of Justice Programs (OJP)

- Bureau of Justice Assistance (BJA)
- Bureau of Justice Statistics (BJS)
- Office for Victims of Crime (OVC)
- Office of Juvenile Justice and Delinquency Prevention (OJJDP)
- National Institute of Justice (NIJ)
- National Criminal Justice Reference Service (NCJRS)
- National Law Enforcement and Corrections Technology Center (NLECTC)
- Office of Professional Responsibility (OPR)
- National Drug Intelligence Center (NDIC)
- U.S. Parole Commission
- Department of Treasury
- Bureau of Alcohol, Tobacco and Firearms (ATF)
- State Department
- Bureau of Diplomatic Security
- Bureau for International Narcotics and Law Enforcement Affairs
- Counterterrorism Office

Uruguay

- Ministerio del Interior
- Poder Judicial

Venezuela

- Ministerio del Interior y Justicia
- Cuerpo de Investigaciones Científicas, Penales y Criminalísticas

- Oficina Nacional Antidrogas (O.N.A.)
- Servicio Nacional Integrado de Administración Tributaria, ente encargado de la administración de las Aduanas.

RECRUITMENT

Approximately 550 staff members from more than 80 different countries are employed at the INTERPOL General Secretariat, regional bureaus and the liaison office at the United Nations, working in any of the organization's four official languages: Arabic, English, French and Spanish.

A third of these are either seconded or detached by their national law enforcement administrations in INTERPOL's 186 member countries; the remaining are international civil servants hired under contract directly by the organization.

INTERPOL accepts applications from nationals of all member countries to ensure that the organization remains truly representative.

Values

With such a diverse group of men and women, the organization's values play a particularly important role in maintaining a harmonious and effective working environment. The INTERPOL General Secretariat defines its values through the following qualities:

- Respect for human rights
- Integrity
- Commitment to quality
- Availability
- Team spirit

- Value for money
- Accountability

Fundamental Competencies

Competencies are the set of capabilities (incl. knowledge, skills, experience, values, behaviour and attitudes) required to perform effectively in a post.

6 Fundamental Competencies have been defined by INTERPOL and are applicable to 'all' staff regardless of their function/grade within INTERPOL. This aims at indicating to the applicants the type of basic competencies which are expected from them, in addition to the requirements specified in the vacancies.

Bibliography

ADKINS, CHARLES: *Late 19th and Early 20th Century, Cartridge Case Analysis, in Alaska*, Fairbanks, University of Alaska, 1997.

ALBERT, M.J. AND OELBERG, H.F.: *How to Load Primers for Small Arms Cartridges*, Elkader, Idaho, 1944.

ALPHIN, ARTHUR: *Any Shot You Want; The A-Square Handloading and Rifle Manual*, Pewee Valley, Kentucky, 1996.

BARLOW, WILLIAM: *Notes on Ammunition*, Stationery Office, London, U.K., 1872.

BARTLETT, WALLACE: *Cartridges for Small Arms*, Pioneer Press, 1985.

BAYLEY, DAVID H.: *Police for the Future,* New York, Oxford University Press, 1994.

BEARSE, RAY: *Centerfire American Rifle Cartridges, 1892-1963*, Barnes, Brunswick, New Jersey, 1966.

BITTNER, EGON: *The Functions of Police in Modern Society,* Chevy Chase, Md., National Institute of Mental Health, 1970.

BLYTH, DON AND DUNN, ANTHONY G.: *The .22 Rimfires of Canada,* White Pigeon, Michigan, 1991.

BRATTON, WILLIAM J.: *Turnaround: How America's Top Cop Reversed the Crime Epidemic,* New York, Random House, 1998.

BROWNE, CHARLES: *Ammunition for Rifled Ordnance*, London, U.K., 1870.

CHAMBERLAIN, R. H.: *Early Loading Tools and Bullet Molds*, Porterville, California, 1988.

CORSI, RICCARDO: *Guida per L'Identificazione Delle Cartucce*, Firenze, Italy, 1990.

DALLAS, DONALD: *Holland and Holland - 'The Royal' Gunmaker: The Complete History*, Quiller Press, Shrewsbury, U.K., 2003.

ELKS, KEN: *Ammunition with Arabic Markings*, Collector Cartridges, Kingston, U.K., 1979.

FRANCZYK, GRZEGORZ: *Polska Amunicja Strzelecka 1919 – 2004,* Navigator Press, Krakow, Poland, 2004.

GARDNER, ROBERT: *Small Arms Makers*, Bonanza, New York, 1963.

GORE, AL: *Common Sense Government Works Better and Costs Less: Third Report of the National Performance Review*, Washington, D.C., Government Printing Office, 1994.

GRACIA, BARRY: *The Colonial Ammunition Company Cal. .303" Cartridges*, Garcia, Stratford, New Zealand, 1984.

HALEY, KEITH: *What Works in Policing: Operations and Administration Examined*, Ohio, Anderson Publishing, 1992.

HAMMER, MICHAEL, and CHAMPY, JAMES: *Reengineering the Corporation,* New York, Harper-Collins Publishing, 1993.

HARRIS, LYNN: *A List of Cartridge Headstamps for Collectors*, Wellington, New Zealand, 1962.

HOGG, IAN: *Illustrated History of Ammunition*, Quarto, London, 1986.

LANGWORTHY, ROBERT H.: *The Structure of Police Organizations,* New York, Praeger, 1986.

LANGWORTHY, ROBERT; HUGHES, THOMAS; and SANDERS, BETH: *Law Enforcement Recruitment, Selection, and Training: A Survey of Major Police Departments in the U.S.,* Washington, D.C., Academy of Criminal Justice Sciences, Police Section, 1995.

MAGUIRE, EDWARD R.: *Context, Complexity and Control: Organizational Structure in American Police Agencies,* Albany, N.Y., SUNY Press, 1999.

MASTROFSKI, STEPHEN D.: *Policing for People,* Washington, D.C., Police Foundation, 1999.

MCDOWELL, BRUCE: *Evolution of the Winchester,* Armory Publications, Tacoma, 1985.

MURPHY, PATRICK V., and PLATE, THOMAS: *Commissioner: A View from the Top of American Law Enforcement,* New York, Simon and Schuster, 1977.

OSBORNE, DAVID, and GAEBLER, TED: *Reinventing Government,* New York, Addison-Wesley, 1992.

OSTROM, ELINOR; PARKS, ROGER B.; and WHITAKER, GORDON P.: *Patterns of Metropolitan Policing,* Cambridge, Mass., Ballinger Publishing Co., 1978.

PEAK, KENNETH, J.: *Policing America: Methods, Issues, Challenges,* Upper Saddle River, N.J.: Prentice Hall, 1997.

REAVES, BRIAN A., and GOLDBERG, ANDREW L.: *Census of State and Local Law Enforcement Agencies, 1996,* Washington, D.C., Bureau of Justice Statistics, 1999.

REAVES, BRIAN A.: *Local Police Departments, 1993,* Washington, D.C., Bureau of Justice Statistics, 1996.

SENGE, PETER M.: The Fifth Discipline: The Art and Practice of the Learning Organization, New York, Doubleday, 1990.

SONES, JAMES: United States Registered Trademarks for Ammunition and Powders, Denver, Colorado, 1992.

WALKER, SAMUEL: *Popular Justice,* New York, Oxford University Press, 1980.

WEISHEIT, RALPH A.; WELLS, L. EDWARD; and FALCONE, DAVID N.: *Crime and Policing in Rural and Small-Town America: An Overview of the Issues,* Washington, D.C., National Institute of Justice, 1995.

WILSON, JAMES Q.: *Varieties of Police Behavior,* Cambridge, Mass., Harvard University Press, 1968.

WILSON, ORLANDO W.: *Police Administration,* New York, McGraw Hill, 1963.

WYCOFF, MARY ANN, and KELLING, GEORGE L.: *The Dallas Experience: Organizational Reform,* Washington, D.C.: Police Foundation, 1978.

INDEX

D

J

L

T

U

V

W

❑❑❑